PRAISE FC
CHAOS

“Apart from my wife’s cheesecake, I know of nothing more binge-worthy than a good book. And when it has been baking in the creative minds of my friends at InScribe, so much the better. This anthology is proof that their talent pool is deep and wide.”

— PHIL CALLAWAY, BESTSELLING AUTHOR AND HOST OF LAUGH AGAIN RADIO

"Life hurts sometimes, but God has woven hope into our DNA. Thanks to writers willing to share and make themselves vulnerable, this book shows us how expressing our creative gifts plays a role in healing our hearts and helping us discover beauty in our pain.”

— GRACE FOX, SPEAKER AND AUTHOR OF *NAMES OF GOD: LIVING UNAFRAID*

"We all have our stories. We’ve faced challenges, crises, and struggles in life. This anthology illustrates how using our creative talents contributes to the restoration of our spirits. Whether through poetry, reflections, or creative nonfiction, this collection offers inspiration and hope in trying times.”

— KIMBERLEY PAYNE, AUTHOR OF MEETING FAITH DEVOTIONAL SERIES

"It takes courage to be creative, because the very nature of the process means trying new things that are sometimes messy, and yes chaotic. The outcome in this anthology truly shows the worth of all these brave and wonderful and breath-taking ventures."

— SIGMUND BROUWER, AUTHOR OF *THIEF OF GLORY*, CHRISTY AWARD BOOK OF THE YEAR

"CREATIVITY & CHAOS is an exceptional collection of work by various authors. What is most remarkable is the amount of diversity in this anthology coupled with the high degree of writing quality. There's no doubt in my mind that many readers will find pieces that are fascinating, inspiring, and entertaining, whether in fiction, nonfiction, poetry, devotionals, or any number of other categories."

— MURRAY PURA, AWARD-WINNING AUTHOR OF *THE WINGS OF MORNING*, *MAJESTIC AND WILD*, AND *STREAMS*

"This book is a cozy meeting place at the intersection of Faith Avenue and Tough Times Street. You will find beauty, encouragement, and overcoming hope in these pages."

— DAVID KITZ, CHAIR OF THE WORD GUILD AND AUTHOR OF *PSALMS 365: DEVELOP A LIFE OF WORSHIP & PRAYER*

CREATIVITY & CHAOS

ARTISTIC ENDEAVOURS FOR TRYING TIMES

INSCRIBE CHRISTIAN WRITERS' FELLOWSHIP

25+ YEARS OF INSPIRING WRITERS

InScribe Press

Creativity & Chaos: Artistic Endeavours for Trying Times

Cover design: 99Designs

Interior design & Layout: Ruth L. Snyder

Managing Editor: Nina Faye Morey

Anthology Team: Nina Faye Morey, Ruth L. Snyder, MaryAnn Ward, Brenda Leyland, Tracy Krauss, Marnie Pohlmann, Carol Thornton, and Lynn J. Simpson

All photos by photographer's name unless otherwise credited.

Published by InScribe Press, https://inscribe.org

Printed in Canada by PageMaster Publication Services Inc., https://pagemaster.ca

Paperback ISBN: 978-0-9940405-6-5

Ebook ISBN: 978-0-9940405-7-2

CONTENTS

PART SIX
MEMOIR

PART SEVEN
POETRY

FOREWORD

I'm sure all of us have experienced turbulent times of some kind when all that is normal either no longer exists or is no longer effective in helping us cope. Times of grief cause our cognitive function to vanish. Sudden changes in circumstances or environment leave us disoriented and groping for some kind of foothold. Sickness takes hold and leaves us feeling helplessly drained.

Giving up and staying in bed indefinitely, though it may seem appealing, is not an option.

In these well-written pieces, the authors share their experiences and the often surprising ways in which they learned to cope with their chaos through creativity. The variety of their solutions speaks to the uniqueness God has bestowed on each one of us.

The experiences are varied and distinctive, but there is a universal thread that ties them together and makes them accessible to all. Whether it was playing with building blocks, turning to crafting, or spending time in "a rustic little cottage on the edge of a marsh," creativity became the outlet that led to renewed mental and spiritual stability.

Some speak of the need to cling to our Saviour through the well-known avenues of Scripture reading and prayer, but some admitted even those one-time sources of blessing were dry and no longer helpful. Seeking other ways to sense the reassurance and comfort of God opened new perspectives and new pathways into His presence. All of these pathways were revealed to be gifts from God's hand in the end, proving the truth of James 1:17: "Every good and perfect gift is from above, coming down from the Father of the heavenly lights, who does not change like shifting shadows."

These are stories that give us encouragement and hope. For when we find ourselves in those times of chaos and disruption, we will remember them and take heart, for we know we are not alone. God has not abandoned us. Others found a way to creativity amidst chaos and so shall we.

Marcia Lee Laycock
Award-winning Christian Writer & Speaker

INTRODUCTION

On this 25th anniversary of the formation of InScribe Christian Writers' Fellowship (ICWF), it is my honour to write the introduction to our fourth InScribe Anthology, *Creativity & Chaos: Artistic Endeavours for Trying Times.* There is no question that in recent years we have all gone through trying times, including a global pandemic. In a way, this book is a natural outgrowth of what we have come through. In this volume, you will see how people use their creativity to cope with the difficult and chaotic times in their lives, whether they be personal or global trials. When you read the diverse selection of stories, poems, and essays contained here, you will be amazed at the accounts of creativity born and crafted in the context of chaos.

Many thanks to Nina Faye Morey, Press Coordinator and Managing Editor, under whose competent leadership the InScribe Press team laboured diligently. Early stages of the project involved the Board in voting on the wonderful cover designs presented by *99Designs.* This was a fascinating experience for those of us new to publishing. Volunteers all, the InScribe Press team then began the process of selecting pieces, editing, formatting, design and layout, proofreading, marketing, and promotion. Several team members wore multiple hats in this process. Thanks go to Nina Faye Morey, Ruth L. Snyder, Brenda Leyland, Tracy Krauss, Marnie Pohlmann, Lynn J. Simpson, Carol Thornton, and MaryAnn Ward for the many hours of work they dedicated to this project.

For 25 years, ICWF has been "*stimulating, supporting, and encouraging Canadian Christian writers in the advancement of their writing so they can effectively minister to others, promote Christianity, and contribute to the public's appreciation of the arts.*" In this volume, you will experience some of the fruits of our efforts. If you are a writer who wants to develop your skills and share your stories, please visit www.inscribe.org and consider joining our fellowship.

We hope, dear reader, that the book you are holding will be an encouragement to you for difficult times you may face. Each of our contributors and volunteers are committed to glorifying God with their talents. Our prayer is that the God who spoke into the chaos of darkness and created all things will be glorified through this creative offering.

Barbara Fuller
President, ICWF

PART ONE
FICTION

Dandelion by K. Payne

A STONE GHOST

VALERIE RONALD

Owen stood on the sidewalk in the shadow of the church steeple and let out a wry laugh. It felt odd exiting his throat, reflecting the dark irony in his purchase of this derelict church. Owen Noble and church were as opposite as oil and water; however, the building did meet his requirements for a spacious sculptor's studio. Besides, this backwater town held few reminders of his wife, Enid, to ambush him at every corner.

Owen could not deny the air of tranquility he felt when he stepped through the heavy double doors of his new studio. Met with a faint aroma of long-dead flowers and the echoes of countless old hymns, his eyes were drawn to the rose window above the dais. The stained-glass depiction of a risen Christ with outstretched arms made him uneasy. The window would have to be sold.

Much of the building needed work, but its bones were sound. He liked its bones—age-darkened wood beams curving in ribs above him, oak panels lining the walls, interspersed with tall windows framed in Gothic arches. Devoid of pews and pulpit, the sanctuary's airy dimensions would soon showcase the substantial proportions of his sculptures. They were still packed in crates, waiting for unveiling when the dust of renovation settled.

The rhythmic pounding of a hammer came from behind a large crate. He shook his head. Past six and Jackie was still here. After one more wallop, his jack-of-all-trades appeared, grinning at Owen from under a dusty ball cap. Her steel gray curls attempted escape, as did a matronly figure from paint-stained coveralls. The best carpenter around, Jackie Houser was his one friend here. When small-town eyebrows were raised at a sculptor moving into the old church, she showed up at his door with her toolbox and a chocolate cake. She did everything, from helping him pitch out decades worth of church debris to rewiring the outdated electrical system. She was also a good listener, or so she told him.

"Hey, boss. Just a few more popped floorboards to anchor down and I think we're done. Time to let these ladies out of their boxes."

Jackie patted the crate behind her. Owen sensed how curious she was to see the larger-than-life figures he sculpted. She never inquired, but he guessed he was an enigma to her, a brooding artist who kept to himself. Handing her the coffee he brought, he felt something give deep down. Dust motes floated around him in the amber light filtering through grimy windows, never coming to rest. Like him. He had floated too long. *Why not now? Why not Jackie, someone who wasn't there when my world fell apart, who never knew Enid?*

By the time he told his story to Jackie, their coffee was cold.

"So, every figure I sculpt has a bit of Enid in it. She's been gone five years but it's like she's in the stone, just waiting to come out. Sometimes there is a lift of the shoulder or an arch of the foot, that is Enid. I don't know how it happens. I never used her as a model when she was alive, yet she forms under my hands like a stone ghost."

Jackie probably wondered why a man his age was already gray around the temples and lined in the face. Now she knew. Elbows on his knees, he stared at the floor, waiting for her to say something. She rested her hand on his shoulder. When Owen finally looked up, her eyes were warm upon him and a small, sad smile curved her lips.

"There is some love that needs to finish its business, even after death. Maybe Enid comes out in your sculptures because she still has something to say."

He jerked his shoulder away from her hand.

"How could you know that?" Owen snapped.

Locked up inside him all this time, he had finally let the story out, only to have this woman peel away the debris of years in a few sentences, like a bandage stripped violently from a wound.

"Five years is a long time to leave the door shut, Owen. Perhaps it's time to listen to what she is trying to tell you."

After Jackie left, he grabbed a crowbar and began tearing into the largest crate in the center of the room. With each rip of splintering wood, he felt anger surge in his blood. Enid's face in those last days filled his mind, skeletal yet radiant with some inner light. He could almost hear her weak whisper.

"He is coming for me, Owen. To take me to be with Him. I'm not afraid. You could know Him too. He will help you when I'm gone. He has gifted you to make beauty. Make it for Him—for God."

How could he accept a god who snatched her out of his life, who let her decay in a hospital bed, who allowed her bright spark to be snuffed forever?

"No!"

Another board fractured under the crowbar, clattering to the floor.

"No!"

Blood dripped down his hand from a deep splinter, but he kept hacking. With a final wrench, the crate fell away.

"No."

He exhaled a last denial, his chest heaving as he leaned on his knees before a figure swathed in packing paper. She had been in a crate for a long time, since Enid died. He had not been able to look at her, this stone woman formed out of the crucible of his suffering.

Since Enid's final prognosis, he had chipped, carved, and smoothed each limb, each feature, until the sculpture was perfect, the best he had ever done. Upraised arms so life-like they could be warm to the touch, hair stirred by a breeze almost felt, and a mouth ready to speak a word at any moment. He called her "Soul," the Welsh meaning of Enid's name.

Now he felt an urgency to release her from her paper shroud. The room grew gloomy with the onset of evening, yet he kept working, carefully unfurling the lengths of wrapping until she stood free before him, a spectre in the dim light. He ran his hands over her arms, down her arched back, making sure she was not damaged.

As he circled the statue, splashes of colour began to appear on her white skin. Blues and yellows and soft reds glowed in random shapes across her stone robe. He traced the source of colour back up to the rose window set high beneath the arch of the ceiling. A brilliant moon sent its cool white light through the jewel-coloured glass, bringing the image of Jesus alive on the surface of the sculpture.

Owen felt the hair stand up on the back of his neck. Where the stone woman stretched out her arms, the arms of the stained-glass Jesus met them. Spots of crimson floated on her hands; the marks of crucifixion superimposed on each palm. A translucent gold circlet hung on her pale brow above eyes overlaid by dark Jewish eyes.

He slumped to his knees before the sculpture, transfixed, until the moon rose higher in the night sky and the colors faded. Then he felt something release within him, a stirring, a breaking, a desire for what he could not name. From his knees, he fell to his face.

Owen stood back while Jackie studied the sculpture bathed in the warm light of morning.

Walking slowly around it, his friend shook her head in wonder.

"You have a great gift, Owen. She is so beautiful, so life-like. And I like that you gave her a small imperfection."

Jackie smiled as she indicated the stone woman's ears.

"You made her ears a little pointed."

Owen did not recall deliberately putting something of Enid in this sculpture, but there it was. Enid's ears had been a little pointed. He reached up to caress the carved ear, recalling his wife's gamin face laughing up into his when he teased her about them. He felt his lips curl up in a full smile; the first in many years.

"I've changed my mind about the rose window, Jackie. I'm going to leave it right where it is. Enid would've liked Jesus watching over me."

Then he gave a small, solemn nod to the figure in the glass.

A Changing View

GRAEME CONNELL

Spring Flowers by K. Payne

I'm looking out the door of my garden cabin this morning hoping to see something. Yep, just something—anything, really. As a writer, I'm always expecting to see something. Even if it is not there. My view today is the same as yesterday. Pleasant garden beds, flowers on the way, or flowers past. Seasons. Orderly and predictable to the display enthusiast. Low plants at the front, larger at the rear, early blooms, late blooms. Makes sense. But I was hoping to see "something," even learn something. Like, wouldn't it be great if a dinosaur poked his head over the white vinyl fence? I imagine he'd be too big to fit in the yard, even to plonk his great foot on the small section of green lawn. Now, that would be something to see, perhaps write about. Or, if I squinted a bit harder, maybe I'd spot an angel sitting on an imaginary stool under the oak tree. That would be a jaw dropper, especially if I knew what an angel looked like. It would take my breath away for sure. Probably more than say the three, or is it four, claws of a Tyrannosaurus rex mitt mid-lawn.

I look back at my laptop, my fingers poised over the keyboard, hoping for a gentle rush of inspiration. But my eyes return to the garden where there is order and there is peace. Perhaps an angel will show if I think hard enough, maybe close my eyes. Now I'm wondering why I want to see an angel close up in the peace of the garden. I suppose it might be because the garden has seen and heard a surge of angst and unpleasantness of late. The fence and, therefore, the garden could not withstand the blustery wind hammering into this blissful place. What a mess.

Far, far away, rockets explode their way into homes and factories, uprooting trees and destroying lives. There are angels scrabbling through the rubble. I just know it. They are sorely needed in that unwanted turmoil of human stupidity. Faith labours to calm the wounded in the shadows and makeshift shelters.

While my lips are loath to say, "I want," I pray and plead for settlement in these global pockets of terror. Will we see an end to suffering and displacement when flowers, yellows, reds, and blues, once again blossom and green trees stand erect and strong in the existing fields of horror and chaos?

Dream on, buddy, I'm told. Dream on. I wonder, too, so close to home, the structured march to recreate our planet and heed the advice of the learned. Have decades of reaping the resources forever ruined our climate? Our land? This place we call Earth—the land and its oceans—

ringed high above by an outer shroud of whirling, chattering contrivances of the modern age. I have to wonder how much space remains in that outer orbit. Somewhere I read there are currently about 8000 satellites circling the earth, and each week it seems a new one ba-rooms aloft, almost as reliable now as the mailman putting an envelope in my mailbox.

The diesel engine roar and the bang-crash of the garbage truck in the lane circles me back to the garden and what I hope to see. A squirrel, unnerved by the noise, descends the oak and sits quietly on the steps, nibbling at his harvest. He's a curious fellow and a regular guest outside my garden cabin. It wouldn't surprise me if I see him burying a few spruce cones later. Maybe in the petunias.

The raucous squark of a peripatetic blue jay shakes a new quiet of our suburban arboretum. No doubt he'll be down on the steps once he's checked the place out. A newly-fallen acorn might just make his midafternoon snack.

Do these new scenes have anything to do with my "something"? I can gaze out my door all day, hope on one hand, zippo on the other. Will I see hope, even? Who, what, where? And when will inspiration and motivation move into view?

Silly questions in today's context. Roll back a few decades and I can just about nominate the hour that hope did arrive. Fresh hope, fresh energy, a quiet heat coursing through every cell of my body. A clear voice calling deep within to come, "Come to Me." Forgiveness for a life being lived where no man should be. I find renewal. I am refreshed.

There's a bird bath in the middle of our garden, surrounded by tall purplish liatris on one side and pink flourishing veronica on the other. Blue jays, magpies, chickadees, crows, robins, and red-breasted nuthatches quench their thirst there. Some decide on a bath, water spraying everywhere. Bees scale the floral tips of the flowers. The garden is a modest place of action.

I cringe when clippers and secateurs, spade and trowel, resculpt the garden beds for next year. The bold and beautiful remain; some suffer a trim. The brash and colourful short-termers give their seed to sprout next year.

For writers, our actions move from words to sentences. We're attentive to the inner voice. Take heed and compose. To ignore is folly, as brilliance and ever-changing light oversee any trek through dark woods. Thriving in the garden rests with the hand that fashions beauty from disorder, where one flower brightens the gloomiest corner.

Did I see an angel? Nope. Yet I know there was at least one. An hour later, there's a wee ripple through the leaves of the mountain ash, the elm, and the oak. I know, without a doubt, that I can sing about angels watching over me.

I whisper a quiet, "Thank you, O Lord, my God. You are always with me," and return to my laptop garden. I feel a presence in my cabin as my brain notifies my fingers where to press the keys. I love it. This is the magic, that I can add words to a sentence, the sentence to the paragraph, which graciously assembles with others into scenes and onward into a chapter and more till sometime hence I can borrow the quote: "That's a wrap."

The paragraphs gather, and a story comes together, as does the garden. As the season unrolls, the soil fades from view under the bright-coloured faces of the annuals. The words assemble as pollinators move around, delighting in the blooms as they appear. Out of the calamity of a writer's work, extra words find opportunity in the paragraph.

I think back to the inspiration of my first novel about explorer Dermot and the outcome of his long, solitary, dark Antarctic winter. Then came widower Brewster sharing his passion around wildflowers in a second novel. Not surprising then to find Brandon in my third novel suffering the return of his childhood polio virus and finding his modern life in a berry and vegetable garden. And what about Theo in the fourth novel and how a "something" gave him a new life? All characters came through some personal crisis. They all found a "something."

Today, the blooms in the flower garden are stable in their surroundings, but laptop Cartwright, my emerging character, wants only to know where he belongs. A plane crash violently interrupted his childhood. I write. Life moves him to his mid-twenties and I must find his answer. I watch the blue jay who has burst into my afternoon. I feel a nudge from the presence in my cabin. Can this noisy bird be the catalyst for Cartwright's peace?

I move our character to a new location to pursue his desire to belong. A fashionably distinct bird emerges and, through the artistic style of magical realism, urges Cartwright to resolve a strange mystery. I outline his twists and turns for solace, new pals to move through his seasons, and his joy at successes. I've plotted a route to halfway, where Cartwright experiences a mild, false victory. The challenge is what propels the story over the top for a successful conclusion readers will enjoy?

The liatris and veronica will backdrop next year's attraction. The poppies will happily reseed and belong, but the garden bed loses the cheerful faces of the marigold. Cartwright will reflect on his 15-year pilgrimage. Moreover, as he believes he is a child of the living God, he can stamp the soil underfoot and know that he belongs.

Vibrancy outside my cabin, increased tumult in foreign parts, and my character finds his answer. Will these forces coalesce to produce the script for a contemporary novel? The flowers respond to the gardener's care; the story responds to the editor's care; the writer responds to his creation.

Like Cartwright, our characters negotiate their paths through calamity and opportunity to realize God's love gives rest, peace, and belonging to those who turn to Him.

Now, what's that massive hoof-print in the middle of our lawn?

After the War

STARLA KLINGER

The cemetery was covered in a deep red with golden light feathering its rays along the flowing lines of the poppies. The skyline was a calming blue broken up by the tombs of soldiers who had sacrificed their lives. An overwhelming sense of sadness filled Emily's heart as she walked the rows of graves. She had memorized the location of her brother's tombstone and had saved for years to make the journey to see his resting place in France. She would not rush this opportunity and took her time as she walked along the rows of soldiers, each one representing someone loved and brave, forever buried in a foreign land.

Her brother was only nineteen years old when he answered the call to serve. It seemed so unfair at the time. How could he go and leave Mama and her alone on the farm? Father had died when they were younger, and her brother had taken on the responsibilities her father had left behind. Her brother had shared his heart with her one evening as they watched the sun set over their crops. "It's eating away at me, Emily, to see my friends enlist and not join them. This is something I have to do. Something I feel God calling me to do." On the day he left, he embraced her and whispered in her ear how proud he was of his little sister. Waving from the train he shouted to her and Mama that he loved them. That was the last time they would hear his voice or see his youthful smile.

Taking a deep breath, she walked along the row that led to her brother's grave. Kneeling in front of his tomb, she ran her fingers along the inscription carved into the stone. "A Soldier of the Great War, Nathaniel Bond." A shiver ran through her as the cold of the stone met the warmth of her fingers. Mama had given her father's comb to place at the base of her brother's grave. For some reason, he had cherished that comb, and he would have it now.

Pulling out her journal, Emily sketched the tomb, along with the surrounding area, to show her Mama when she returned, since Mama was too sick to travel. Drawing was something she was good at, and she often made some extra coins sketching portraits and landscapes at the town market. She saved these coins until she had enough to travel to her brother's resting place. As she closed the journal, the memory of her brother giving it to her came to mind. "You're a great writer, Emily. Would you write everything that happens while I am gone and read it to me when I get home?" A single tear ran down her cheek and dripped onto the cover. Writing in the journal had helped her process the death, sadness, and hard times surrounding her and those in her community.

Emily reached to pick a poppy from the field next to her brother's grave. As she did, she heard the faint sound of marching boots. Lifting the flower to smell its fragrance, she instead could smell gun powder and mud. Looking around, her eyes took in the cost of war. The poppy brought to her senses the battle from her brother's perspective. Opening her journal, she placed the poppy amongst the pages. She would save this piece of history.

Emily began to tell her brother stories of all that had happened at home since he had been gone. "Not long after you enlisted our farmhands did the same. Mama and I were left to manage the farm and bring in the crops on our own. One night, while Mama was at her quilting group, the other women were sharing how they, too, were left without anyone to help with their farms, businesses, and shops. When she came home that night, she passed me a piece of paper with a schedule on it. The quilting group had come up with a plan to help every family who needed it. Their plan had worked well, and all the crops were brought in on time."

Emily went on to share about the strain on the economy and the community as resources became fewer and the deaths of loved ones became more frequent. "Mama didn't get out of bed for months when the news of your death reached us." Wiping a tear, she continued. "I was heartbroken but had to grieve you in the quiet of night in my room. I had so much to do to make sure we didn't lose the farm. Thankfully, you and Papa kept records and notes of all I needed to know.

"Eric Miller returned home a few months after the news of your death. He lost his hand during the war. It was hard to see a boy I went to school with come home as a wounded man. Mama gave him a job on the farm when no one else would hire him because of his injury. Turns out he is an excellent bookkeeper and businessman, which has allowed Mama to hire some new farmhands.

"When news reached us that the war was over, the town threw a huge celebration with a live band and dancing. Eric asked me to dance, and it was wonderful. The town created a monument in the park and held a beautiful service when the last soldier came home. Your name is on a plaque, along with all the others who perished in service to our country. I stop at it each time I am in town and say a prayer."

Emily continued to share stories until the sun began to set and she knew she needed to leave. Rising to her feet, she looked at her brother's tomb one last time and said in a tear-filled whisper, "I love you, Nate." Turning away, she began the walk back to her hotel, feeling a sense of closure. She would remember him. Looking around the cemetery as the evening light cast shadows on the tombs of her fellow countrymen, she told herself that she would remember all of them.

PART TWO
CREATIVE NONFICTION

Growth is Possible by Shannon Erickson

LESS THAN A CARPENTER

MEG TYSOE

Daffodils from Canva Pro

I bought this wreck of a house against all wisdom, but at the time, I'd been homeless for a year. When I came upon it through the sleet of that hopeless February morning, masses of daffodils were blooming by the door. Battered flat, it's true, on the muddied, snowy earth, but defiantly green and gold. Daring me.

Long ago, I'd come to see my life as a house. All my hopes and energies loosed and lost on bricks and plaster. On the frescoes of my wistful artistry.

The first "house" of my marriage was a trailer. My autistic son and I—overcoming—painted the fake wood walls with mucky fingers, copying from a book the ochre and red art of Lascaux. Stags and bulls; cats and horses. My ambitious husband, whose office hours usually went to midnight, only saw our Lascaux by tranquil candlelight. I've always been sorry he couldn't join us on the hunting trails of ancient Dordogne, where we roasted wild beasts in forest clearings and ate hamburgers cooked on our rusty Coleman stove.

There were "real" houses after those trailer years, and more frescoes. A hammock in a piney wood, designed when I couldn't walk to where the live trees grew.

"Leave Canada," my neurologist said, when a tendency to clumsiness was diagnosed as multiple sclerosis. "Go somewhere warm and dry." And so, the Côte d'Azur became my overseas sanatorium.

Once, in the viridian light of a sirocco, I painted the kitchen wall of our new home with a view from outside—the sea below Roman ramparts, lashed to fury by hot desert winds, sending waves into our courtyard to crash on the madly flowering bougainvillea. I worked in a flurry of shredded pink confetti.

The peace there was unfathomable. Two books, three, four were spawned over the years, in between visitors—mostly clients of my successful husband. I saw hardened, brittle executives, even determinedly blasé teens, shattered by the release of unexpected tears. Mourning doves crooned from tiled rooftops. Cliff swallows soared and darted and called to the sunrise. Coming outside with coffee, one always brushed against lemons or rosemary—the enduring fragrance of Provence.

I painted lavender on the courtyard wall with poetry from the Song of Songs (2:12; 4:16): "Flowers appear on the earth; the season of singing has come, the cooing of doves is heard in our land . . . come, south wind! Blow on my garden, that its fragrance may spread everywhere." I wrote in French, so most people needed a translation. Often, that meant sharing the Word with believers and unbelievers alike. These many years later, I still can hear the strumming of a guitar, murmurs of prayer and laughter, along with the seaweed tang and rich smells of roasting Sisteron lamb with garlic, saturating so many velvet nights.

Then came the day when, around my kitchen fresco, I drew words of the poet Supervielle. "When no one is looking at her, the sea is no longer the sea; she is what we are when no one is looking at us."[1]

No one will ever look at me again. The words choked any clear thought. It seemed that "for better or worse" no longer included fried myelin and its twitchy spin-offs. What God had joined, a man had put asunder. My man.

But God. My Saviour. His eye is on the swallows. On the daffodils. Surely, surely, He's watching me?

The place of beloved exile—my home for twenty years—was gone. Life became cold winters again, bed and breakfasts, here a night, there a week. Living out of a knapsack, on tinned tuna and a prayer.

"Write," friends said. But the words were penned up in the dark layers of my battle-shocked mind. I wrote and missed deadlines. I took a publishing contract and failed to launch. I limped on, at length, to the ruin of a house in the woods. Splatted daffodils.

But through the icy drizzle, a sloping vineyard stretched to the ends of vision. And, not so distant, there was water. Not the Med, but Lake Ontario, passing itself off commendably to eyes aching for the Blue Coast.

Here I could live again. Art and a stone fireplace. Vine-clad pergolas, fields of lavender—or at least a bee-busy garden of it. Provence and enchantment—not only for myself but for anyone with a soul needing sustenance to shine again.

Isak Dinesen, whose *Out of Africa* set me on course as a writer when I was ten, said the cure for everything is salt water—sweat, or tears, or the salt sea.[2] God already had a wineskin full with my tears. The sea was far away. But sweat? There was no doubt about sweat in my future.

I've sweated for seven years.

In the beginning, tearing down crooked walls, levering up rotted wood and cracked tile floors, so much sweat stung my eyes that I saw nothing clearly. It took a brother in Christ to show me how bitter and narrow I'd become. So, for a while, I turned my back on the rubble and refaced the colossal, ugly fireplace with stone. I mixed mortar and dreamed of company, blizzards raging but bright firelight inside, the smell of woodsmoke, cinnamon and hot cider. I imagined Christmas—a balsam fir filling the great bow window, the house redolent with wintry resin instead of grit and varnish fumes. I saw my son and his wife stringing up fairy lights, arguing amiably about carol music by Sting.

But no. Not yet.

There was a flood. Squirrels, it transpired, had made my weeping tiles their storage depot. Monsoons came, and the fountains of the great deep burst open. Billions of walnuts spattered over the rising waters. Days of pumping left a clay sludge on everything—including my soul.

It took me almost as long as Noah to get over that little episode. Sans ark, I drowned within.

Before the flood, I had begun a fresco. It was still there, forgotten in the chaos. One morning, I read about beauty for ashes, and I remembered.

It was a view over the Med from a place where I had written several books. I thought about those days, sitting on a bed of sun-warmed pine needles, bare tanned legs dangling over a rocky ledge to the sea. Words tumbling out so fast I could scarcely capture them in my salt-stained notebook.

I've spent long nights over the years gazing at that fresco in candlelight that hides all the jobs yet undone. Inevitably, when someone sees it for the first time, they say, "You must have been very happy there."

Danger lurks everywhere when your life has been shattered. Seemingly good things birth new regrets, even despair. For this I keep the apostle Paul on my desktop: "Forgetting what is behind. . ." (Philippians 3:13b). We all know the words. This, Paul tells us, is a mature faith: "Only let us live up to what we have already attained" (Philippians 3:16).

More sweat. The rebuilding of walls. After almost three years, a real bathroom and a kitchen. No more doing dishes in the tub.

I built the massive kitchen island of acacia wood. The cutting and the placing, the sanding and the finishing, of every board brought me into the presence of my Saviour. This house—this *home*—I was building to Him. It was my tabernacle, my ark of the covenant, and my table of offerings. Overlaid not by pure gold but by my sweat. By my blood—because I'm much less than a carpenter. In the centre, I made a stone fountain to remind me that the Lord Jesus has replaced the Gihon spring with living water.

I said earlier that I saw my life as a house. If a dwelling can be a metaphor in this earthly journey, perhaps it's because we're designed as godly alchemists to transmute that *Imago Dei* in us to something tangible. Our gold is art—not merely in paint and words but in wood and stone and food and fires.

I look back now on the communion of years and see it not as random moments of beauty, snatched amidst the ugliness of life, but as all of life itself. The knocks and bruises, the floods and losses, are all jumbled in a glorious mess with my son's painterly hands in mine and memories of a husband's touch, though now he belongs to another. My place as a child of the Life Giver, the Logos, must be to break through the veil between this hard life and transcendent reality, however painful the effort. To show forth the glory in the flower, even when it's dashed in frozen mud.

"The anguish of the singer," wrote Sadie Williams, "makes the sweetness of the strain."[3] This—as I cringe at my still-unfinished walls, yet thumbtacked there are photo proofs of love, of life—this I know is our burden; this is our joy.

THE POWER OF PRAYER

LORRIE MORALES

My cell phone buzzes. One more annoying interruption as I sit at my computer working on my latest writing project, my memoir.

I am drawn back in time. It is late. The phone has not stopped ringing. The family congregates in our parents' cozy living room. It is normally a place for celebrations. But tonight, we are drawn together by potentially devastating news. My red-eyed, teary mother kneels beside her bed begging God to save her prodigal son, Charles. My siblings have assembled after traversing various parts of the country to console each other. My younger sister wanders into the kitchen looking for something to feed the clan or perhaps distract herself. My older sister stands in the sunroom staring into space, a cigarette dangling between her slender fingers. Another brother stands in the hallway, speaking quietly to his fiancé on his cellphone. My father lies back in his Easy-boy chair, eyes closed, longing to shut everything out, especially these people who have invaded his peaceful space.

Suddenly, the front screen door opens, letting in a gust of chilly night air. My older brother tiptoes in like he's afraid of stepping on broken glass, when it's hearts that are in danger of shattering. My sister peeps in from the kitchen and rushes to him, burrowing her face in his shoulder. The others greet him, too, and my father opens his bloodshot eyes.

I am one of these family members he sees. I am the creative, contemplative daughter who has boxes of diaries, journals, short stories, and doodle pages stashed in drawers in my office and under my bed. Dealing with this latest interruption to our lives has me madly journaling, trying to make sense of this stressful situation.

I have driven all day to be near my parents and siblings. Now, I am sitting in my parents' stuffy house on their well-worn couch beside my brother, who reeks of cigarettes, alcohol, and burnt toast. We are waiting for the doctor's call. They've been operating on Charles for hours.

"Perhaps it would be best," my mother suggests as she emerges from her prayer room, "if we all try to get some rest and wait until the morning to learn the news." I know she will be awake all night, praying that her son survives. We have never doubted our mother's faith. And so, honouring her wishes, we all gravitate to various beds and couches to get some sleep before the morning.

Laying on my back, staring at the ceiling, a thousand thoughts racing through my mind, I call on the name of the Lord to save my brother. I reach for the thin, worn New Testament in my purse and open it to the Psalms. David's cries are mine, too. I composed a poem in my worn journal.

Charlie has always been a wayward son, a prodigal, and a troubled soul. He'd become an alcoholic, moving from job to job and trying different addiction centers before moving back home to live in my parents' basement. He'd finally moved into his own apartment and pretended that everything was "fine" until he told his employer and friends that he had cancer. Then he'd given away his possessions, tidied his place, and wrote the note he left for my parents. His lies, the addictions, and his choices have cost us more than dollars and time. And yet, here we were, rallying together to see if the medical profession could save his very life—the one that Jesus loves, too, I thought.

Heaven knows where Charlie found the gun. The police said it was a miracle he was able to crawl up the ditch from the blood-splattered car and still raise his hand. The woman who saw that hand never usually went to the mailbox on Thursday, but she did that day. She called 911, and the helicopter was on its way back from a call just minutes away. I know the prayers of a righteous woman were heard, and God orchestrated every event that day.

That horrible night was not the beginning of my brother's story or of our family's constant prayers, but of the realization that I had a story inside me that I needed to tell. So, early in the morning after my devotions at the kitchen table, I got the urge to find my journal and a pen and fill the pages with words, adding to the thoughts already scrawled across the pages.

As I began to write, I recalled my six-year-old self, standing by my mother's hospital bed. I only knew it was her because of her eyes. Pregnant with my brother, her head had smashed through the front window of our car in a head-on collision. Her face was bandaged in white, but I knew her touch. I remembered the doctor saying I could draw her a picture because her eyes were not damaged. I somehow knew she was going to be all right. My sisters and I suffered concussions, and my father sustained a scratch. My oldest brother had internal injuries and was rushed by air ambulance to a bigger hospital. I was too young to know mom still had a baby living and breathing in her womb. Little did she know she would spend a lifetime praying for Charlie throughout other life-and-death scenarios.

Little did I know I would take on my mother's prayer role and become an author and artist.

Recently, I got a call from Charlie. I had continued to see him off and on for several years and kept tabs on him after my parents passed on. He was finding it a struggle to pay the rent and his health was failing. "Perhaps," he asked, "Could I stay with you for a while?"

I have had my own problems throughout the years. But rather than alcohol, I cried tears and took up painting, drawing, and art classes at the Art Centre. My friends supported me with coffee, conversation, and junk journal mornings. I bought a sketchbook and drew out my feelings. I joined Bible studies and worshiped with women of faith at my church. I even started a devotional blog on my website. Most of all, I continued my mother's fervent prayers for Charlie, along with my other siblings. And I continued to write. I published my first book, then a second, and finally a third. I also knew that I was the answer to Charlie's prayer.

I may never know why God spared Charlie's life on so many occasions. But I do know that the power of prayer is still evident as God continues to provide, rescue sinners, and use me as His servant. I do not know what the future holds, but I continue to praise the God who created us and gave us talents and gifts. I give Him the glory for all He has done and continues to do in our lives.

Here I am today with a stronger faith, a love of Jesus, and a peace about what happened so many years ago. There are still other stories inside my head waiting to be told, printed, and shared with others, as well as other books sitting in files on my computer. I will continue being prayerful and creative because, "There is a time for everything, and a season for every activity under the heavens" (Ecclesiastes 3:1).

GREEN COTTAGE MERCIES

VALERIE RONALD

God Cares by Shannon Erickson

"Here's the key."

Karen pressed it into my palm, her hand warm around mine.

"It's a place where you can get away for a few days. I want you to use it like it's your own."

My friend's invitation to stay at her little green cottage while she went on a trip was a lifesaver. She knew I desperately needed a reprieve from the constant stress of this chaotic time in my life. Overwhelmed by a difficult divorce as well as a recent cancer diagnosis, I longed for a place of peace and calm where I could catch my breath.

It was not fancy—just a rustic little cottage on the edge of a marsh—yet it was exactly what I needed. Karen struggled to single parent her young daughter on a limited income, but she still managed to create a home of peace and charm. I stepped through the door, welcomed by a bouquet of wildflowers and a brightly coloured child's drawing on the kitchen table. Then I dropped my small bag on the floor and crumpled into a chair, finally able to cry. There was no one here to see my tears fall.

My life was a maelstrom. Neglected and abandoned by my unfaithful husband, I was now the focus of his vindictive campaign to leave me broken and destitute. In the middle of the fight, I was diagnosed with non-Hodgkins lymphoma, a slow-moving cancer treated with a "watch and wait" approach. This went against every fiber of my being. I wanted the killing disease dealt with immediately, but the doctors thought differently. God was my calm center in the eye of the storm. The more the tempest raged, the more I sought His safe lap of love. God's attentive ear and compassionate heart heard it all. I felt no shame in crying before Him.

Tears drying on my cheeks, I aimlessly wandered from room to room, then outside to the garden. Would I someday find a place of refuge and beauty as Karen had here in this little green cottage?

I longed to, yet my future loomed uncertain and cloudy. Did I even have a future when poverty threatened and cancer stalked my veins like a predator? I found it hard to feel hope in the bleakness of it all.

Sleep overcame me that first day. The quiet consoled my exhausted body and mind, beckoning me into the forgetfulness of slumber. The next morning, birdsong and gentle sunlight woke me from a deep sleep, the best I had experienced in a long while. Where I lived in the city, the constant din of traffic took a toll on my nerves. Here, the peaceful sounds of nature soothed them like a healing balm.

After breakfast, I sat outside in the warm sunshine with my Bible open in my lap. I couldn't concentrate on reading for long, just a few verses at a time on which to meditate. But I wanted to know—what did Jesus say about rest?

I found an answer to my question in Mark 6:31: "Then, because so many people were coming and going that they did not even have a chance to eat, he said to them, 'Come with Me by yourselves to a quiet place and get some rest.'"

Jesus gave this invitation to His disciples after an intense time of ministry. I took it to my own heart as Jesus bidding me to step aside from the chaos and to come away with Him by myself to this quiet place of rest. I closed my Bible, resting my hands on its worn cover. This was all I needed for now—quiet, rest, and Jesus, my beloved companion, closer than my own breath.

It was restorative to sleep and eat when I needed to, go on gentle walks, and take time to pray and read, yet I wanted something to do with my hands. Although I had not painted for a long while, I decided to dust off the neglected brushes and watercolours I had brought with me. My ex-husband used to belittle my desire to write or paint, but he no longer had the power to make me feel guilty for expressing myself creatively.

I set up my few art supplies on a weathered picnic table near the garden. The nearby flowers offered up their beauty as delightful subjects, so I picked a few to put in a mason jar on the table. Without thought of technique or skill, I applied liberal strokes of fresh green, sunny yellow, and poppy red to the paper. Creating art released a calm within me. I marvelled at God's imagination as I studied the intricate design of every flower. Gazing at each unique bloom, capturing their delicacy and colour, put me in a place of peaceful focus. Breathing became easier, my shoulders relaxed, and my heartbeat calmed. Before I knew it, several paintings were drying on the table.

In the simple act of watercolour painting, God flowed His inspiration through my eyes, my heart, and my hands. The paintings were not masterpieces, but they made room for an intimate part of my soul to come alive again. I felt an unfamiliar sense of accomplishment that carried me through the evening in a lighter mood.

The next morning, I packed a small lunch and a journal in a bag and drove to a nearby beach. The ocean waves washing rhythmically on the sand and the fresh salt breeze ministered to my sore heart like a healer's hands. Down the deserted beach, I found a sheltered place between the rocks and logs, where I sat contemplating the sea view.

The previous day's painting session had opened a restoring stream of creativity in me. I had been plodding through for so long, my head down, trying to find enough strength for each step, that it never occurred to me to spend time on an activity I genuinely enjoyed. For years, I was made to feel guilty when I attempted painting or writing, so I quit trying. I believed I did not deserve to do something that gave me joy, just for myself. I was wrong.

Now my fingers itched to put pen to paper as well. A place where the jumble of my thoughts and feelings could distill into words. I poured my heart out, page after page—all the hurt, anger, rejection, fear, and loss. Then, gradually, the words became a prayer written directly to Jesus. Line after line, I described the beauty before me—the ever-changing blue of the sea, gulls soaring above like graceful dancers, shaded layers of sand, water, mountains, and clouds—made by Jesus, originator of all things. Eventually, I put down my pen, wordless in wonder and adoration. I knew with certainty that my God, Creator of all I saw before me, would also create a way through the wilderness for this stumbling child of His.

My retreat at the little green cottage was a watershed time during those traumatic years. I wish I could say that everything improved from then on, but that would be untrue. The divorce continued to cause deep stress for my family, and the cancer required surgery and many months of chemotherapy. Through it all, I returned often to watercolour painting and journaling, creative practices that gave me an expressive outlet for all the emotions bewildering me. Looking back on what I created during that time, I see beauty rising from ashes, joy despite mourning, and the spirit of praise amid heaviness. To the feet of my Creator, I came in brokenness with my small offerings of praise, worship, and love. God knew how to bring creativity out of my chaos, beginning a healing journey He still leads me on to this day.

PART THREE
NONFICTION

Look to the Heavens by Shannon Erickson

JOURNALING THROUGH CHAOS

RUTH KEIGHLEY

My heart rate rose as I gripped my pen tightly and began transferring onto paper what was burning in my heart. My journal described the pain, horrifying memories, and the progressive hope of spending eight weeks in addiction rehabilitation. Somewhere, deep inside, I was aware that if I failed to work hard or gave up, I would not live much longer. Suicide would be my only option.

I was a recovering alcoholic and had just been diagnosed with bipolar disorder. I was married with three young children, and rather than providing a safe, comfortable place to live, I had created a home that included physical and emotional abuse.

The time I spent in the rehab centre was only three weeks. By the end of that time, I was left feeling raw and exposed. There was no way I was able to go home and pick up my duties as a wife and mother. Fortunately, I was able to go into a halfway house for five weeks, and there I was able to heal enough to step back into the real world once again, even though it was with uncertainty and hesitation.

For eight weeks, I kept up a journal expressing my rage, resentments, failures, inadequacies, hopelessness, and longings. The more I wrote, the more vulnerable I felt. It was a release to get all these things out, but the thought of anyone finding and reading those journals made me feel anxious. I sure didn't want my family to ever read them. I didn't want them to learn that I resented being a mother and wished I could be rid of them all and be able to do my own thing, even if it meant destroying myself.

When our daughter was fourteen, she was taken from our home and placed in foster care because I beat her up. That was one of the darkest days of my life. When the car drove away with her watching me through the window, I fell across the table and screamed until I could no longer make a sound. After being transferred to different foster homes over the next several months, she ran away and lived on the streets, where she stayed for two and a half years. She fell through the cracks and didn't get the help she should have received.

Those were some of the most devastating years of my life. Again, I poured my heart onto the empty page as I tried to understand how my life had deteriorated so badly. Tears dampened the paper as I penned words of grief and fear. I'm sure I cried myself to sleep every night for those three years. Journaling helped me sort out what was happening and how it was affecting me physically, emotionally, mentally, and spiritually. It helped me stay on track as I wrestled with my faith and sought to find God's hand in all that was happening.

Over the next several years, our family went through turmoil. I spent a lot of time in the psych ward, and my husband and kids tried their best to manage. I felt like such a failure. It seemed to me that the kids were getting used to me not being there, and they were raising themselves. Even when I was home, I struggled with being there emotionally for my children. I was so caught up in my own pain that I didn't know how to ease theirs. At times, I felt that the kids resented my presence, and I felt left out and incompetent.

All through those years, I loved the Lord and sought hard to walk with him. Yet, I couldn't understand how a Christian could experience the agony of mental illness and the consequences of the disease. Was mental illness truly just sin in my life as so many fellow Christians were telling me? Was it possible to be a Christian and an alcoholic too?

I continued to write in my journals and pour out my heart to the Lord. I found that the process of journaling had a healing effect. It helped me to calm down and take the time to examine my motives and, at times, irrational thinking. I came to realize that I had to take responsibility for my own behaviour.

Yes, I had a mental illness, but I could not use that as an excuse to be selfish and unreliable. Never could it give me license to be abusive. Never could it give me a valid reason to hurt myself or others. Yes, God is the healer, but I had to submit myself to Him and allow Him to work in my life. It has been a painful yet profound journey. It drew me ever closer to the God, who guided me safely through that journey.

Gradually, I began to heal. The Lord never did take away my bipolar disorder, but I began to put the survival skills I had learned into practise. I learned how to recognize the symptoms of an advancing depression and take the steps I needed to stop the downward progression. I became aware of my limitations and took the necessary steps to avoid situations that would compromise my ability to prevent the disease from becoming a major setback.

I gathered all my journals I had kept secret and used them to write a book, *Healing for an Unquiet Mind.* I omitted some of the deeply personal thoughts and feelings that would hurt my family and included everything that revealed my story with integrity. After I wrote the book, my husband lit a fire in our fire pit, and I destroyed all those journals. They represented a past that I had recovered from and wanted to leave in the past. Burning those journals gave me a sense of freedom and released me from the hold that the past had on my life.

Writing the book was therapeutic and allowed me to move forward in my new-found freedom.

The journey is not over yet, but I move forward with complete confidence that the Lord is in control and will remain with me to the end of the journey. I continue to write in my journals, but they now express not only the difficult times but also the increasing positive times and the faith that has developed into full submission to my Lord Jesus Christ.

CANCER, CHAOS, AND CREATIVITY

NINA FAYE MOREY

Just before my 58th birthday in 2010, I received a diagnosis that made me all too aware of life's chaotic twists and turns. I'd experienced many ups and downs throughout my lifetime, but this was a season of my life during which everything seemed to be going well. I had a job I enjoyed, great friendships with my colleagues, a wonderful marriage, and excellent health—or so I thought. But suddenly I was faced with the prospect that my happy, healthy, peaceful existence was about to abruptly end. I'd contemplated doing and enjoying so many things in a future that appeared infinite, but now I was forced to confront the transient nature of my worldly existence. Perhaps I'd been flying too high, and now it was time to have my wings clipped.

Once my family doctor and oncologist suspected I had breast cancer, they put me through a whirlwind of tests. These included a mammogram, ultrasound, CT scan, MRI, and breast biopsy to determine the stage, my prognosis, and the best treatment options. Although fearful, I tried to remain upbeat throughout this battery of tests, hoping that the final diagnosis wouldn't be as bad as first thought. But once I received a devastating diagnosis, I was thrown into emotional turmoil. My future instantaneously felt indefinite and uncertain, and I was stricken with feelings of helplessness and hopelessness. Cancer had seized control of my life.

Once I commenced treatment, which was a year-long journey for me, it was a busy time of going to the cancer centre for rounds of chemotherapy, then the hospital for surgery, and finally returning to the cancer centre for a series of radiation treatments. At first, I think I suffered from shellshock. But once I got past that stage, I struggled to remain optimistic. The evil one is always on the lookout for opportunities to inflict pain, desolation, and hopelessness. I fought a daily battle against anxiety, fear, and depression, struggling to maintain some hope and faith in the face of everything my increasingly frail body, mind, and spirit was experiencing.

Fortunately, however, I've always been a fighter. It wasn't long before I became determined never to permit despair to dwindle my hope or diminish my faith. I soon developed a mantra I repeated several times a day to strengthen my resolve and buoy my spirits: "I am a lion. I will devour the cancer; it won't devour me!" I also found comfort in repeating Psalm 23:1-6 whenever I began to feel anxious and fearful. I searched for biblical passages on the power of prayer and God's promises for healing (Matthew 7:7-8; Psalm 107:20; Jeremiah 30:17). I prayed daily for peace, strength, healing, and a quick recovery. I appealed to family, friends, and fellow parishioners, as well as other Christian ministries for prayer to aid in my recovery. I recited this prayer from my *Catholic Book of Prayers* daily:

> *O Sacred Heart of Jesus, I come to ask You for the gift of restored health that I may serve You more faithfully and love You more sincerely. I want to be well if it is Your will and redounds to Your glory.*
>
> *If on the other hand it is Your will that my sickness continue, I want to bear it with patience. If in Your divine wisdom I am to be restored to health and*

strength, I will strive to show my gratitude by a constant and faithful service rendered to You, my loving Savior and Redeemer, and my God.

I placed myself in God's hands, and He became my constant companion, providing a much-needed source of strength, hope, comfort, and peace. Even when my body felt frail, I remained firm and steadfast in my faith and refused to give in to despair.

I came upon an anonymous quote that assures believers that, "Where there is hope, there is faith; where there is faith, miracles happen." In Matthew 9:20-22, Jesus affirms the miraculous healing power of faith when he tells the diseased woman, "Take heart, daughter, your faith has healed you." There are many pathways on the journey to healing, but the various remedies offered by earthly physicians can lead us down a confusing road to recovery. Ultimately, there is only one true way—our Divine Physician proffers a single path to healing physically, mentally, emotionally, and spiritually.

Once I laid my fears at the feet of God, I immediately felt more empowered and optimistic. Instead of allowing my weakness to turn me into a worrier, I resolved to become a warrior for wellness. I began keeping a gratitude journal to help me stay focused on the positive aspects of my life. It helped me to see that despite all the negativity, God granted me many daily blessings. I became more aware and appreciative of all these positive gifts instead of dwelling on life's negatives. It felt wonderful to once again "seize the day." My renewed ability to envisage my future uninhibited by worry or woe was truly liberating for both my soul and spirit. Jesus exhorts us not to worry for it will do nothing to lengthen our life (Matthew 6:27). Many recent scientific studies back Him up, suggesting that indeed worrying seems to reduce life expectancy.

Reading the Lord's Word reassured and restored me, providing me with the willpower to prevail in the face of disease, adversity, and infirmity. I meditated daily on Scriptural passages that encouraged and empowered me. I started a spiritual journal, recording passages where I felt the Holy Spirit comforting my soul and consoling my spirit. I found journaling a powerful method for dealing with my painful thoughts and feelings. Soon my journaling restored my urge to write, which I'd abandoned during my long road to recovery. I began posting these comforting verses by my computer for daily contemplation and inspiration. The Lord's Word provided the courage to cope with a potentially deadly disease and peacefully accept the precariousness of life (John 14:27). Reading His Word calmed my fears and offered profound insights into the nature of pain and suffering and the mysteries of life and death.

If we are faithful, God promises to use whatever misfortunes befall us for our good. He will save us according to His plan and purpose for our lives (Romans. 8:28). The afflictions we face in this life are the crosses we must bear. In return for sharing in Christ's suffering, we receive an equal share in His eternal glory (1 Peter 4:12-13). The pain and suffering we endure has another positive side. It often acts as a catalyst for change, causing us to search for meaning and purpose, to reexamine and reform our lives, and to turn or return to our faith. It has the potential to transform our pain into possibility.

My year-long struggle with cancer altered my perspective of life. Although I'd been happy with my job, sitting at a desk all day no longer seemed fulfilling. I wanted the freedom to enjoy life. I looked for ways to transform all the trauma, pain, and negativity I'd endured into positive creative energy. Having always enjoyed the outdoors, I began to see anew the grandeur of God in nature. Before long, I wanted to express myself creatively again for His glorification. With renewed purpose, I brought out my pencil crayons, felt markers, and water-colours to paint all the wonderous sights in this world—radiant autumnal leaves, graceful soaring birds, luminous kaleidoscopic sunsets. I sat down at my computer to write about my cancer journey and how it had changed me. I wrote to find my new self in the life that still lies ahead of me. I started composing poetry again. Poetry has a magical way of transporting me beyond this material world into the spiritual and mystical realms. Perhaps more than any other artistic endeavour, it provides the power to tap into my emotions and express my feelings. Engaging in various forms of artistic expression provides solace and sustains me in my daily life.

Now I'm able again to envision a happy, healthy, joyous, and peaceful life stretching out ahead of me. I place my hope in God and try to take advantage of every opportunity He sends my way. I'm forever grateful for the healing power God granted me through His Word and the miracles of modern medicine. I'll never again take the prospect of a long life for granted. I live each day to the fullest, enjoying every extra minute He's given me. Like Mary, I'm content to sit at the Lord's feet each day as He reveals truths to me through His Word (Luke 10:39). He's renewed my strength, allowing my creative fire to burn brightly once more. God's my constant source of inspiration, and I continue to write and create works of art in honour of Him. Despite whatever challenges and chaos life might bring, He has given me the power to spread my wings once more and soar above them (Isaiah 40:31).

Finding True Hope

SHANNON ERICKSON

Finding True Hope by Shannon Erickson

I've always loved photography, but my opportunities to engage in this artistic endeavour dwindled as my young family grew. New rhythms and demands of life took over. Gone were the days of exploring new places, trying new techniques, and finding beauty in the ordinary. It seemed like the chaos of life with a toddler, a babe in arms, and another on the way was enough to derail my artistic passions.

On the day my baby girl was due to be born, I planted my precious lilies. Her arrival came two months earlier than expected, and she had already parted to heaven before I got to hold her in my arms.

My sweet three-year-old daughter had insisted her baby sister be named Lily Blossom. When she arrived, we gave her the name Cassandra Lily Blossom. We thought how special it would be to plant lilies so that we could all remember our sweet angel baby. I was delighted to discover an oriental variety of lilies called the Cassandra Lily. It was a delicate white lily with a soft yellow center. What a beautiful way to remember our baby girl.

The first sight of new growth was exhilarating. In some ways, life was beginning to feel a bit more normal. People could see I was coping better. I don't know how people can go through an experience like this without having faith in God.

The day I saw those red bugs, I thought my heart was breaking all over again. I had never seen these scarlet lily beetles before in my life. This year, they were everywhere. Of course, this was the year I had invested more hope in seeing these lilies grow. The beetles destroyed my precious Cassandra lilies, and it felt like they destroyed me at the same time.

As I processed the tears and deep emotions, both sadness and anger, that this destruction had triggered, I began to consider the "WHY." Why did the loss of these lilies shake me so much? How could I move forward? I had placed so much hope in seeing those lilies bloom, but I learned that my hope was misplaced.

I knew I had to trust that God was with us on this journey, leading and guiding us. But in that moment, I had to question if I had truly placed my hope in Him. I continued to reflect and practice placing my hope in Christ, and gradually my heart began to heal. Once again, I was able to focus on *true* hope. With this new-found hope, my passion for photography was reignited.

In the chaos of life, I had lost more than I realized. Picking up my camera again helped me reconnect with myself, God, and the world around me in a new way. This was the start of fresh artistic discovery. I'd always had the desire to be creative, but I often second guessed my creative abilities. Time and time again, God has brought me back to photography. He's assured me I am creative because He is creative, and I am made in His image.

While my lilies may not have come to fruition the way I first hoped, God did eventually give me my Cassandra lilies, along with fresh hope for our future. I learned to slow down and deeply appreciate the things God has placed around us—reminders of His provision and care. As Matthew 6:30 (NLT) says, "And if God cares so wonderfully for wildflowers that are here today and thrown into the fire tomorrow, he will certainly care for you."

How beautiful that "[w]e can rejoice, too, when we run into problems and trials, for we know that they help us develop endurance. And endurance develops strength of character, and character strengthens our confident hope of salvation. And this hope will not lead to disappointment. For we know how dearly God loves us, because he has given us the Holy Spirit to fill our hearts with his love" (Romans 5:3-5 NLT).

That fresh start has continued as I have learned to take time to slow down and appreciate the world around me. I've also been encouraged to continue pursuing my artistic expression through macro photography by others who have seen potential within me.

I am often drawn to capture the beauty in the natural world through the lens of my camera. From crisp, intelligently designed snowflakes to the elegant flow of lilies, I am reminded of the importance of endurance that leads to a hope that does not disappoint.

I create because of the One who created us and loves us more than we can imagine. I hope my photography can tell the story of divine beauty, endurance, and true hope.

There are always ways to heal.

RECOVERING FROM THE CHAOS OF PTSD

MARNIE POHLMANN

I've spent a lifetime learning to regain balance and health in my life. Living was always a struggle for me. While I've survived, even thrived at times, with God holding my hand, I still struggle.

Before Post Traumatic Stress Disorder (PTSD) became officially recognized, my doctor explained that I suffered with this disability because of childhood sexual abuse. I experienced many common symptoms: missing memories, insomnia, nightmares, flashbacks, rage, loss of self, unhealthy choices, panic attacks, and more. But once I understood what PTSD was, I knew why living was such a battle. Despite a diagnosis and knowing God was at my side, sometimes carrying me, I still fought to be a joyful Christian.

PTSD often occurs when a person's normal coping methods are overwhelmed by either a single tragedy or a cumulative series of struggles. My childhood was the main cause of my PTSD, but other circumstances, many arising from my own choices, also contributed to my failing self-esteem and mental health.

As a child, I'd not yet developed any real coping methods, so I resorted to survival. I was easily influenced by others, trying to gain approval and love. I wore masks every day to hide the pain and shame. Memories, both good and bad, were lost in a dark void to protect me. But either the associated emotions would arise at inopportune times or I'd be frozen while a flashback took over the present.

Unfortunately, as I grew to adulthood, those survival modes remained instinctively active even when situations changed. I've spent many years trying to unlearn these instincts to appear "normal" so others would not see my secrets. I've eventually learned there's a need for instinctual behaviour and no such thing as normal. Though I wouldn't claim my mind is healed, I've learned to name feelings like hunger, sadness, and rage. I've worked hard to relearn to trust others and myself, identify truth from imagined truth, and be vulnerable and honest more often.

There's controversy over the best methods to treat PTSD, from visualization and talk therapy to psychedelic drugs and shock therapy. I found a twelve-step support group for adult survivors of sexual abuse helpful. Finding both common life themes and ladies who understood what I was saying was empowering and provided support as I tried various methods to lessen symptoms. Reading Christian and non-Christian books on the subject was enlightening. There weren't many Christian books then, but today there are many. When I was able, I spoke to professionals. Like finding a hairdresser, everyone needs to find the books and doctors that are useful to them. Many doctors prescribed medications. Anti-depressants didn't help. However, anti-anxiety drugs did help my brain function better, enabling me to make better decisions and progress in the journey. It's worth the risk!

In one season of my life, I was diagnosed with cancer, which led to a body-changing and life-changing bilateral mastectomy. During my recovery, my husband was also diagnosed with cancer. I'm presently cancer-free, while it's a matter of when, not if, his will return. I also experienced Seasonal Deficit Disorder from living in the North, working for years in a basement office. I loved my job assisting police officers; however, this work exposed me to situations that eventually caused secondary PTSD. Then my primary PTSD, which I thought had been sufficiently dealt with, mingled with these other circumstances. Surprisingly quickly, I found myself in a dark hole. Scripture was clear that if I could capture my thoughts, I could be thinking of lovely things, not my struggles (2 Corinthians 10:5). But *how?*

At that time, speaking with a therapist, I learned a skill—a practical way—to be obedient to God while not ignoring the chaos. I was able to look at Post Traumatic Stress Disorder in a new light. I did this by looking at the priorities God wanted for me and reframing the issues, which led to replacing negative thoughts with positive thoughts (Philippians 4:8). I rewrote PTSD from what it is to what I need.

No longer is P for Post

P is for Present

God is present and active in my life today. Although I still need to look at the past, I can now see how far I've come. Rather than feeling like I'm still reliving the past, I live in the present. Even amid current struggles, I'm able to stay grounded in the present with God at my side.

P is for Pray

I can pray and talk with God about anything at any time. God always listens. Especially when I'm quiet, I can hear God speak to me. Prayer is a conversation that clears confused thinking.

P is for Play

I'm allowed to play. Yes, even while I need to "adult." It's acceptable to take time to participate in activities that fill my cup. I can play with words or toy bricks, have spa treatments, or cheer for my favoured football team. (Go Riders!)

No longer is T for Traumatic

T is for Time

Time heals, so "they" say. However, the passing of time doesn't help unless I engage in activities that bring healing. Trauma, even repeated trauma, is only for a moment; yet in that moment, time slows and may create deep scars. Pain and consequences may remain active and repeat as life goes on. It takes time to heal and change when your normal has changed forever.

T is for Talk

Talking—whether with friends, family, or even myself through a journal—is a helpful way to give voice to what happened, name my feelings, and file experiences appropriately so they don't explode in life at inconvenient times. Talk therapy with a counselor, psychologist, or psychiatrist is also an option when talking with family or friends is neither possible nor enough.

T is for Trust

Trust isn't easy when I believe no one understands my words or feelings. Yet as I talk honestly with God and myself, trust grows. Tiny steps and trials show who will safely hold and guard both confidential information and my heart. When I take the time to talk, I can learn to trust my own instincts and discern the truth.

No longer is S for Stress

S is for Sing

I'm not an audiophile and prefer quiet to playing music while I work or write, but music truly is a gift when stress seems overwhelming. From loud singing that wears off anxious energy to humming along to a comforting tune, music improves mental health. Tchaikovsky helped me fall asleep through my teen years. Rock and Roll reminded me of God's presence and love during parties. Hymns and worship choruses spoke to my soul when I needed calm. Sometimes music truly does speak when words are not enough.

S is for Sort

Sorting, at least for me, is a mindless activity. Filing papers or books in numerical or alphabetical order doesn't take much thought and helps me stay calm and productive. Sorting anything from toy bricks to spice cabinets may not lead to a happy life, but cleaning and organizing helps to bring orderliness and tranquility to my chaotic mind.

S is for Simplify

Once I simplify life—most often by knowing when to say no to people-pleasing—my stress levels are reduced. I make choices to do things God asks me to do, not what others ask me to do. I choose to do things that fill my cup with joy rather than drain my energy. It's not easy to obtain a simple life; it takes effort and prayerful consideration.

No longer is D for Disorder

D is for Do

Life happens when I'm not looking. Healing isn't something that happens while lying in bed, avoiding people and life. Doing is part of healing. I must do the hard things. I must face my giants. I need to do activities that energize me. I need to create to truly live—*this* is what brings healing. I can't simply think about it, I must do it!

D is for Don't

"Don't-ing" is just as important as "doing." I must use prayerful discretion about what to do and what not to do. I need to be active, not busy. I need to be productive, not people-pleasing. I must guard my energy for life's important times, those relationships I cherish, and continued healing.

D is for Decide

Deciding what to do and what not to do, then doing what I've decided is the only path forward. Talking to God, and perhaps others, helps guide me. Knowing the difference between good choices and poor choices can be difficult and takes practice. Day by day, I choose what to do and what not to do, and then I practice acting on my decisions.

Just as God promised in Psalm 32:8, He has led me to use these methods to recover from the trauma of my PTSD.

May you rewrite, reframe, and replace the chaos in your life by asking God for new words, actions, and understandings that will lead to the healing of your emotional wounds.

CREATING JUNK JOURNALS

CAROL HARRISON

Ideas flit in and out of my mind like a hummingbird darting to and from a feeder filled with sweet nectar. Each one demands time to be considered. To-do lists fill pages of notebooks as I try and keep track of appointments, daily tasks, and obligations. Jotting them down helps me corral them so they can't escape my memory before I have the opportunity to complete them. Too often the creative ideas grow, but the to-do lists gain the upper hand. The ensuing chaos of projects and lists chokes my creativity. Could I harness some of this chaotic energy to fuel my creative endeavours instead? What form of creativity would enable me to regain balance in my life?

A wise counsellor explained that balance between creative and work aspects of my life comes through engaging in an activity requiring both my mind and hands-on components. This helps pull me away from the stresses of everyday life and its chaos. One suggestion was to play with paper crafting materials as a form of art therapy. I had to wrap my head around this idea of giving myself permission to play with no goal in mind except to enjoy the process. I needed to let go of preconceived ideas and unrealistic, specific outcomes, and simply enjoy the activity.

I began researching how to make junk journals while writing my book *Memory Making Moments.* I started making one and realized the process allowed creativity to flow unimpeded by deadlines or goals. There wasn't a right or wrong way to put together these little handmade journals. Each one is unique, even if they contain similar items.

Junk journals originally consisted only of recycled materials—things saved from going into the landfill or recycle container. Now this title also encompasses the use of scraps from your stash of scrapbook paper and inexpensive bought embellishments. Places like dollar stores offer wide varieties in this category without breaking the budget. My junk journals include recycled materials, such as cereal boxes, book pages, paper bags, envelopes from junk mail or bills, and anything else I can find a way to use. I also incorporate bits of lace, ribbon, paint chips, scrapbook paper, drawing paper, and embellishments like broken jewelry or things from dollar or thrift stores. A file folder, cut down and covered in a napkin decoupaged on to it, becomes a small junk journal once I add pages inside. A cereal box, cut down and covered in wallpaper, becomes a larger journal with a spine and multiple "signatures" (groups of pages) inside. Recycled materials take on a new look.

Junk journals consist of a cover with one or more signatures attached within that you decorate with pockets, tuck spots, tags, and other ephemera. To figure out where to even begin or how to attach the pages within a cover, I watched several YouTube videos about junk journaling and discovered a variety of methods, materials used, and finished products. I learned how to make tuck spots and pockets to store bits and pieces in, as well as how to make tags and other ephemera to add into each one.

I look around the play space I've carved for myself in my living room using a coffee table and love seat and see the clutter, which looks like a giant mess of chaos. Yet this chaotic clutter doesn't create more stress, like the jumble of to-do lists, deadlines, appointments, projects to complete, and life obligations demanding my attention. I can just play in this space, moving around pieces, rearranging them, and choosing what to put on each page. The result of the process is a completed junk journal, unique and different in design, colour, size, and decorations each time.

My journals neither look like each other nor do they look like those in the videos. I felt inadequate at first because my work failed to meet some of the teachers' standards, so I had to go back to the creative process and see what I could learn and gain from that. My junk journals needed to be uniquely my own. I could use whatever pieces of recycled material, paper stash, or embellishments I had around and let my creativity flow. I needed to avoid the comparison trap.

After creating more junk journals, I realized a few things. First, the process of making something from very little pulled me away from the stresses and pressures of everyday life. Second, I felt refreshed as the to-do lists and endless projects faded into the background. Finally, I could return to writing, daily tasks, and appointments with a renewed sense of accomplishment and creativity. Simply allowing myself to play and be involved in the process of finding balance through hands-on creative endeavours brought relief from everyday chaos.

I've continued to expand my repertoire of junk journal styles. Now some have spines and multiple signatures. Others are thin and more like an oversized card. The covers and décor of each one is different. There isn't a right and wrong choice, just a process. The end result is a creative piece needing a home.

As I trusted God to help me find the necessary balance in my life through this form of art therapy, I relaxed and enjoyed the play process. The balance my counsellor described between the brain's thinking and physical activity began to emerge. With this balance, my mental health improved. I began to let go of unreasonable expectations I'd placed on myself to strive for unachievable perfection and set my sights on excellence instead.

Even though this has been and still is very good for my mental health, and the creativity spills over into my writing, I still sometimes question myself about the validity of continuing this process. How many junk journals, no matter how different, does one person need? What should I do with all the ones I've made and others I want to try making? I've given several away to friends and family. I've had the opportunity to sell a number of them, especially in conjunction with craft/book sales, and I get to explain how they tie into my *Memory Making Moments* book.

Offering them for sale has given me the chance to hear other people's impressions and what they might want to use one of the journals for in their own life. One lady bought a large one to capture sayings and thoughts from her grandchildren, copy out favourite recipes, as well as jot quotes or her own thoughts. She planned to call it her "everything book." Another person planned to add more cards into theirs. From this storehouse, they could gift others notes of encouragement. The ideas for using them are as different as the people purchasing them and the books themselves. Creativity manifests itself in the making and using of them.

I still have moments of doubt about how much making them, or other forms of art therapy, helps. Is it just a way to procrastinate about other important things? Are my junk journals any good, since they don't look like ones I've seen for sale on Etsy or YouTube? But I keep coming back to create more, trusting God to give me wisdom to know when to play and when to work on other obligations, interests, or projects. I continually need to step back from my own plans and allow God to work out the balance as I find out how creativity can manifest itself in my life even during chaotic times.

TRANSFORMING DARKNESS INTO LIGHT

CAROL THORNTON

There are people who cope with the chaos of grief, heartbreak, or despair by reaching for a paintbrush or pen. In the year of her divorce, Mexican artist Frida Kahlo painted *The Two Fridas*. Two versions of Kahlo sit side by side, their hearts exposed. One heart appears healthy; the other is cut open and bleeding. She painted through her pain.

In her poetry, American Jane Kenyon confronted her life-long depression. Later, while Kenyon was dying of leukemia, her husband, Donald Hall, wrote about what life would be like after she was gone. It became his collection, *Without*. They both wrote through their challenges.

The night two transit company peace officers found my daughter walking on the train tracks after midnight, I didn't reach for my pen. I got in the car with my husband. Crying, hoping, worrying, and, mostly, praying, we drove toward the city sixty miles away. The transit station was a further twenty miles. Would she still be there?

Two weeks later, my daughter (I'll call her Rachel) is safely ensconced in a residential recovery program. I'm still processing the experience, and I want to believe she'll be okay. For now, I can take a breath and reflect on a mother's journey when a family member is in the grip of addiction.

On the night of the call, Rachel had completed a week-long detox program. We hoped this might be the beginning of a new life for her, but treatment programs are oversubscribed, and there would be a five-day delay before she could take the next step to recovery. Transitional housing spaces were full. We were afraid to have her return home to troublesome contacts, and the detox centre agreed to let her stay a few more days.

Three times I called to ask if she was happy to stay longer, and three times the call was disconnected. I thought she was refusing my calls and decided to give her time to cool off. (It turned out a poorly trained worker had accidentally cut me off.) When Rachel thought we didn't want her to come home, she felt trapped and rejected.

That evening, we learned Rachel had discharged herself. The centre couldn't give us more information because of confidentiality rules. Reluctantly, I called her boyfriend, the same guy who'd been abusive throughout their relationship and even threatened to "come over and slit your cat's throat, your mom's throat, and your dad's." He believed she'd contacted a dealer and taken a bus to the city. Nearly paralyzed by fear, I called my friend who's prayed for Rachel for years, and more recently, daily. She prayed with us over the phone line. "I keep seeing a picture of Jesus, and He's saying, 'I am here.'"

Just then, our other phone rang. It was Rachel. "I'm in the city. I just need a few hours on my own. I'm going to stay with a buddy." She was alive. She sounded like herself. I could breathe again.

I phoned our friend to reassure her. She said, "If you need to, call me again, even if it's in the middle of the night."

It was about one thirty in the morning the first time the transit officers called. "We have your daughter here. She's severely intoxicated. She says she wants to come home. We should be shutting down the system, but we'll keep her company until you can get here."

We raced along the highway, curving around mountains in the dim light of a waning crescent moon. As we drove, I took up my friend's offer; the phone call woke her. "I'll be praying. Travel safe."

About the time the road flattened out, the officers called again. First the unsympathetic one who, it seemed, would happily watch a train slam into Rachel.

"Your daughter has walked off; I don't know where she's gone. There's nothing we can do." I pictured her wandering drunk and defenseless, and probably afraid.

Then the voice of the other man. "I'm going to get in my vehicle and drive around. I'm a dad. I'm not giving up. We'll find her. We'll take care of her till you get here."

At two thirty, he called again. "We found your daughter." I breathed a prayer of thanksgiving. There was still hope. "She fell a few times on the rocks, and she's scraped up a bit. We've got her in the vehicle. She's not happy about it." In the background, I could hear Rachel kicking and pounding at the door. I couldn't hear her voice.

He continued. "We found an empty pill bottle on the ground. We don't know if it was hers, so we've called an ambulance."

By the time we reached the station, the medics had been and gone. All they found in her system was alcohol; she hadn't taken pills. She had declined a trip to the hospital.

The reluctant transit officer stayed on the far side of their vehicle. My husband thanked the other man. "We were very blessed that it was you who found her. I think we've met an angel tonight." The words seemed inadequate. He hugged the man awkwardly.

We helped a sobbing Rachel into the car. "I'm sorry I'm so difficult. I'm so sorry."

On the drive home, she rocketed between expressions of rage and of remorse. There was no time to write. I was too busy trying to keep her calm and praying she wouldn't jump out of the moving car. But she'd been writing. She read to me from the journal she'd kept at the detox centre before things went so horribly awry.

The poet David Whyte compares a time like this to a meeting of two storm fronts, when we tread a path between the things that overpower us from outside and those that overwhelm us from within. Sometimes I'd cried out to God. "Where are You? Why aren't You answering my prayers?" But always, after the initial fear and frustration, I knew God was watching over Rachel, and He loved her more than I ever could.

We got home about five in the morning. I did not write that night. First, I took time to soak myself in gratitude that my girl had been found by someone who committed himself to caring for a young woman when she did not love herself enough to want his care. I expressed my gratitude to the benevolent God who loves her. And loves me, even when I feel despair.

Then in the small bright pool cast by my bedside light, I read until my body felt warm again and my mind was calm enough to sleep. As the young Franz Kafka wrote, "A book must be the axe for the frozen sea inside us."[1]

That night was like so many during my daughter's addiction years. I went to sleep. I dreamt, as I often dream, that I was searching for her in a broken building—making my way gingerly through a shattered window, climbing stairs with missing steps, and squeezing through blocked passageways. I woke up cold and shaken, afraid this was the moment when she'd done something that couldn't be undone. When I can, I pray in my own words. But too upset for words to come, I said the Lord's Prayer again and again. " . . . Thy will be done, on earth as it is in heaven . . . deliver us from evil . . . ."

The next morning, I did finally write, but not in an organized way. I threw thoughts, fears, hopes, and questions into my journal to clear my head enough to face the day.

I know when more time has passed, I will wrestle to make sense of the chaos that threatened to overwhelm us all. A phrase or image will appear like a doorway leading to a poem. It might be the lean coyote we saw as we searched for our daughter, knowing she had no money, no phone, and the night was cold. The animal paused in its delicate meander and looked at us as if it wondered about our presence. Or a story might spring from the reflection Rachel saw in the mirror the night she thought her partner might really kill her this time. But these things won't happen right away.

Two weeks after our frantic drive, knowing my daughter is safe for now in the recovery program, I can pick up my pen and pay attention to myself, using my art to process in my own mind the journey I've been on.

Still, I hope and pray that one day I'll be able to write about how the events of a terrible night led Rachel to a complete recovery. Perhaps my words will reach across space and time to touch another mother whose life feels like it's falling apart and let her know she is not alone. God is with her. Then this present darkness will be transformed into light.

THE REALITY OF LIVING THE DREAM

TRACY KRAUSS

Many creatives dream of a stress-free life. Endless days of painting in the outdoors. Writing the next great novel from that desk tucked under the eaves while gazing out the open window at a pastoral landscape. There are no chores to do or meals to prepare in these dreams.

Reality looks quite different. Flies buzz around the easel. A mosquito lands, smudging wet paint. Butt cramp from sitting too long is a real thing, folks! And the view? Who knows? The curtains are drawn to keep the screen glare down.

Our dreams are not always as advertised. Unlimited time and freedom can transform them into something that's quite opposite. Rather than becoming more productive, it's easy to become lazy with too much time and ease on our hands. We get complacent. Procrastination sets in. Why do today what can be put off until tomorrow? Without external motivation, inspiration takes a vacation, leaving blandness in its place. *Might as well just watch TV and wait for the muse to return another day.*

To some degree, we need challenges—even adversity—for the creative juices to kick in. Pressure, seemingly impossible deadlines, honest feedback that sometimes hurts—even outright rejection—all serve to enhance the creative journey and help us grow. Personal trials are often the very inspiration needed to produce work we would never have conceived on our own. Just like fertilizer adds nutrients to the soil, so "chaos" helps the creative process flourish.

Creativity stems from a sense of unrest—a place of desire that needs an outlet—not the endless contentment that the dream perpetuates. Without that sense of unrest, there is no need to create. Some of my most productive times as an author have been during my busiest seasons while working full time, pastoring a church, and looking after a household. In retrospect, this isn't logical, but having too much time can be counterproductive because it eliminates any sense of urgency.

This actually makes sense. When faced with challenging situations, our brains are forced to think in new and creative ways. Out of necessity—be it deadlines, time pressures, or just the curve balls of life—we must focus in order to achieve our creative goals. We are forced to think "outside the box" and "carve out time," which are little more than empty clichés until we're faced with the choice of giving up or pressing forward. Of course, I am talking about moderate levels of stress, not the kind that causes heart attacks. (Been there, done that!)

There are many practical examples of this concept. Looking after our own bodies comes to mind. Exercise and weight training are forms of stress that make our muscles and bones stronger. When certain pathogens are introduced, our bodies create antibodies that make us more resistant to disease. There are examples in almost every facet of life.

Similarly, creativity is an outlet for our pain, helping us make sense of the world. It brings healing, not only to us but potentially to others as they see our example and are affected by the art we produce. Like the butterfly analogy, something ugly becomes something beautiful and meaningful. Take what the devil meant for harm and use it for good. Allow God to work through your experiences because, in God's economy, nothing is wasted. The most creative—and unexpected—work is often birthed because of deep challenges.

Growing from trials is a common theme in the Bible. In James, it says, "Consider it pure joy, my brothers and sisters, whenever you face trials of many kinds, because you know that the testing of your faith produces perseverance. Let perseverance finish its work so that you may be mature and complete, not lacking anything" (James 1: 2-4).

Barriers can become bridges. Obstacles are just opportunities. Adversity is actually good for the creative process and often results in outcomes we could not have envisioned without those obstacles. We must learn to adjust, adapt, and evolve because this is where true creativity lives. Embrace mistakes, failures, and difficulties as fertilizer for growth.

Living the dream is still possible, but it might include some unpleasant circumstances or uncomfortable situations. That's reality. Accept it. Embrace it, even. Stop living in a constant state of dissatisfaction because the world isn't perfect. Only then will true fulfillment come because reality is more desirable than the dream. Let God do something beautiful through you.

TORN LAYERS AND THE HEALING BALM

MARION GRACE

As Christians, we are all familiar with the biblical concept of times and seasons. The book of Esther teaches *"for* such a time as this," and it often brings comfort during life changes and challenging times (Esther 4:14). But what if your trying times are so life-altering, devastating, and debilitating that you are knocked off your feet and can barely lift your head to breathe? What if everything you know and are seems stripped from you?

This is a topic that, though painful, is dear to my heart because I went through and recovered from such an experience. My heart cries out every day as I see the evidence of so many struggling to cope with and recover from life's difficulties. I am compelled by the compassion of Jesus to share with transparency what it was like and how God used some hidden treasures within to restore my value, confidence, and purpose.

When I was diagnosed with final-stage cancer, it was like a whirlwind with all the tests, treatments, consultations, mental bombardment, and drugs. If you have been there, you know that it takes a little while for you to stop spinning and be able to take a good look at what your life now is.

For me, it was a couple of months until the emergency status settled down and I became enveloped with uncomfortable and disturbing thoughts and feelings. I began to see how my body, personality, and abilities had drastically changed. When I looked in the mirror, I saw what I did not recognize—a very altered, depleted, more depressed, and sick-looking woman who had to depend on others for everything. I felt helpless, despairing, and humiliated, not to mention like I was a burden. Everything that made me who I was seemed gone. My marriage was in serious danger, and my heart was broken.

Having always struggled with varying degrees of depression, I recognized the rearing of its ugly head. I knew I was in for the fight of my life. Uncertainty of the future, on any level, can leave us with what feels like a hole in our guts. Perhaps you are there now. When these emotions start to come, you may feel very alone. I know I did. I also felt lost, worthless, and scared. For months, I often found myself crying in a heap on the floor. My identity and purpose seemed to vanish, and I felt like no one really cared or understood.

As I lay in my bed, day after day, I cried out to God for help. I knew He loved me, and I'd read enough Scripture to know that He turns ashes into beauty. I dared to believe that I was not a hopeless case and threw myself fully into His arms. The enemy tried to convince me I was hopeless, but I knew enough about him to know he is a liar. His only purpose is to steal, kill, and destroy (John 10:10), and he revels in chaos.

I had no idea how God could restore me, but I clung to hope. As I spent more and more time in His presence, it began to stir in my spirit to start journaling about how I was feeling, my progress, and what God was teaching me day by day. This was the beginning of discovering previously unknown creativity that would turn into a healing balm and a springboard to a new life. I was very faithful to this, and at one point, my Heavenly Father placed it on my heart to write my journey as a book. Wow! I had mixed feelings of intimidation and wonder, but a sense of hope was birthed in my heart. That's all I needed—God wasn't finished with me.

I was determined and cautiously excited to obey and see where God would take me. As I had no experience or training, I always prayed for at least half an hour before I wrote anything. I wanted to be led by God. Week by week, month by month, I poured myself into my new endeavour and found restoration for my soul. My writing began to unfold as a compassionate, relatable, and encouraging point of connection for many dealing with life's tough issues. As I exercised my gift to bless others, I could not help but begin to reap peace and joy in my difficult season.

I praise You because I am fearfully and wonderfully made; your works are wonderful, I know that full well (Psalms 139:14).

Because we are fearfully and wonderfully made by God, I now picture my life with deep and purposeful layers, like the earth. A lot got peeled off while going through cancer and my marriage struggles, but the creative abilities revealed underneath were just as much a part of me and were always hidden there. God was bringing me into my "such a time as this." I do not believe God caused any of these trials, but He will take what the enemy intended for evil and turn it into good. Don't ever let the devil have anything in your life.

I now continue to use this creative gift to push past negative feelings or problems that arise. It is an opportunity to find an answer from God to share with my readers. I call it "Write, Relate, Inspire."

I want to encourage you to prayerfully seek God about the hidden layers and giftings in you. Different is not inferior, and the whisper of inadequate is a lie. A good place to begin finding new purposes and fulfillment is to start giving back. Start trying things you never considered before, or perhaps were too afraid to attempt. Can you paint, draw, write poetry, speak in a support group you can relate with, start a blog, volunteer at a charity, do crafts, start sharing your testimony, write devotionals, or join a prayer/Bible study group? A simpler way may be to join a class you've always been interested in, perhaps something musical or artistic. You could learn a new language for that dream trip. You may uncover amazing talents and gifts that were hidden till now that could change your whole perspective. Consider these the new layers of the unique YOU. It is a wonderful thing to look at yourself through God's eyes and soar past coping to absolute thriving.

I am not saying it is always easy. I have my frustrating days. I still try things I used to do easily and end up hurting myself. As much as I have learned, I still have a stubborn streak. I used to be called Tigger as a term of endearment, but now I would say I am a cross between Kanga and Wise Old Owl. I'm thankful I didn't turn into Eeyore or Piglet.

We need to focus on God's daily leading and walk closely with Him. Other people's views and expectations may be disheartening, but God is the lifter of your head and the One who gives you value and purpose. He is not surprised by what's happening and can make your life beautiful. When the dust clears, you may be thankful because of who you've become. Embrace your new season.

AFTER GRIEF: RECREATING LIFE FROM THE ASHES

NINA FAYE MOREY

On April 30, 2020, I lost my beloved husband to cancer. The brief forewarning his time was limited left me ill-prepared and devastated by his passing. As I drove away from the emergency department in the wee hours that morning, it hit home that I was truly on my own for the first time in nearly 50 years. I had no idea at that moment what my future life might hold. His death had changed everything.

Despite the pain and difficulties of those days, weeks, and months following my husband's passing, magnified by the COVID-19 Pandemic, I somehow managed to recover and rebuild my life. Like the mythical phoenix, I was able to rise again from the ashes. Ashes have long represented loss and mourning, and the phoenix has symbolized Christ's resurrection and life reborn anew. Like many, I find this symbolism of resurrection, transformation, and rebirth a source of comfort and hope amidst life's crises, chaos, and catastrophes.

But how do we regain hope and begin creating a new life for ourselves after the loss of a loved one? It's no easy feat. There's a subtle difference between mourning and grieving. Mourning is the *expression* of grief we are permitted to exhibit in society for an undefined but *limited* period. However, grief is a very deep, intense, personal, and private response to our loss of a loved one that follows no timelines or rules. It's as unique as each mourner and each person and relationship lost. But what all mourners have in common is that grieving is difficult to endure, and recovery takes time. I know firsthand how grief ebbs and flows. How sights, sounds, and memories can trigger a new episode. How it affects our mental, emotional, physical, and spiritual well-being. Although we must eventually move on with our lives, we never truly get over our loss.

Loss and grief are at the root of much of the emotional pain, turmoil, and upheaval we experience in life. It leaves us searching for meaning. Why did my loved one die? Why am I still here? How can I ever pick up the pieces of my life and put them back together again when half are missing? What will I do with the rest of my life? Finding answers to these questions enables us to move forward with our lives instead of becoming mired in grief. We may find it helps to explore answers to these questions by reading relevant Scriptures and then journaling our thoughts. There is grace and meaning to be found in our grief because of its redemptive power and spiritual significance. To regain hope and joy in our lives, we must understand the deep spiritual meaning of suffering as revealed in the life and death of Christ.

No matter our beliefs, it's difficult to cope with life when our grief feels overwhelming and unending. Don't try to do it alone. Ask for help. Whether or not we have a relationship with Him, God is still there for us. If we seek His help, He will give us the courage, strength, and peace to make it through the day. The Bible tells us that "The Lord is close to the broken hearted and saves those who are crushed in spirit" (Psalm 34:18). Don't hesitate to ask family and friends for help and comfort. They're often willing but may not know how or are waiting to be asked. If we're experiencing anxiety and depression, we shouldn't be afraid to share this with our family physician. They may prescribe medication or provide a referral to a psychiatrist, social worker, or counsellor who specializes in grief counselling and/or Cognitive Behavioural Therapy. There are also free online therapy programs we can take advantage of. My family physician encouraged me to sign up for a course offered by the University of Regina's Online Therapy Unit. I highly recommend Cognitive Behavioural Therapy. It teaches us how to recognize our emotions, accept them, express them in healthy ways, and provides some valuable coping skills to help us deal with the symptoms of our grief.

For believers, faith in God and the afterlife He promises provides a sense of solace and strength during seasons of grief. If we're not already believers, the loss of our loved one may lead us to seek out God for the first time to provide hope, support, and comfort amidst our pain and sorrow. Matthew 5:4 tells us "Blessed are those who mourn, for they will be comforted." However, for some believers, grief may lead them to question their faith in God. They may even blame God for their loss and become angry with Him. If this happens to us, we don't need to be alarmed. It's okay to be open and honest with God. There are numerous examples of people in the Bible becoming angry and disillusioned with God. The Book of Job and the Book of Psalms provide ample proof we're not alone in our anger. It's important we face our anger and deal with it, just as Job and David did. The Almighty is our Creator, and He's capable of both understanding and withstanding our wrath. Isaiah 53:4 attests to this, "Surely he took up our pain and bore our suffering." God is our compassionate Father who listens to our complaints without condemnation. Believers who honestly share their feelings of anger and pain with God will eventually come to experience "the peace of God, which transcends all understanding" (Philippians 4:7).

There is no denying loss and grief changes us. But it's up to us whether we allow those changes to be constructive or destructive. We can collapse under the weight of the chaos grief leaves in its wake, or we can choose to transcend it. How do we arise from the ashes and rekindle our passion for life? We need to accept, respect, and value ourselves; be willing to step out and take risks; and be ready to accept failures and disappointments as well as successes. We need to assume responsibility for our own recovery and invest the time and energy required to use our pain productively to regain our mental, emotional, physical, and spiritual health.

Recovery requires never suppressing or minimizing our hopes, dreams, passions, and ambitions. We need to permit ourselves to explore all options and envision a future that gives our life meaning and significance. Finding new paths through the chaos helps us change, grow, and create. It will be an ongoing process of daily discoveries, new life insights, and spiritual transformation. We must refrain from criticizing ourselves or judging ourselves too harshly as we go through this process. Not everything we try will be an immediate success, but we must be willing to try and to keep on going. It is vital we believe in ourselves. Don't listen to that inner voice telling us we can't. "Yes, we can!"

Hope gives us resilience, optimism, and inspiration and helps us feel more confident and engaged with life. Inspiration sparks our willingness to explore and think "outside the box" for novel solutions to problems. It's the key that unlocks our creativity and motivates us to conceive something new. Creativity has long been associated with mental health. Writers such as Sylvia Plath and artists like Vincent van Gogh have fostered the trope of the "tortured artist." Recent research confirms creativity and artistic pursuits are beneficial to mental health. They provide a positive outlet for people who are experiencing mental and emotional distress. Art therapy has proven especially helpful for victims of trauma. Writing and journaling about painful events has been shown to boost immunity. Engaging in creative activities helps us to get in touch with our feelings and record our cherished memories. It appears engaging in such activities has many positive effects, including reducing stress, anxiety, and depression; improving memory, self-esteem, and coping skills; and increasing healing, resilience, and flexibility. As we channel our thoughts, feelings, and emotions into our creative endeavours, we begin to regain our mental balance and rebuild our lives. Everyone's different and unique, so we must find the creative outlet that works best for us, whether that's artwork, writing, music, drama, dance, scrapbooking . . . the list is endless.

While it can be difficult to express our grief verbally, creative activities help us express our feelings and stimulate and reinvigorate that part of our brain that gives us a sense of hope, joy, peace, and purpose in life. Although it's difficult to imagine doing anything at all after the devastating loss of a loved one, being idle is one of the worst things we can do. Marinating in our own sadness and depression will only feed our downward emotional spiral. Engaging in creative pursuits helps redirect and refocus our thoughts. I found drawing, painting, journaling, and writing powerful outlets for processing my grief. No matter what God-given talent we choose to use, creativity helps us cope with our grief and rise again like the proverbial phoenix. God will give us beauty for ashes (Isaiah 61:3).

PART FOUR
DEVOTIONALS

God Cares by Shannon Erickson

ON REFLECTIONS

LORILEE GUENTER

Orchids from Canva Pro

For now we see only a reflection as in a mirror; then we shall see face to face. Now I know in part; then I shall know fully, even as I am fully known (1 Corinthians 13:12).

As we walk into the Orchid show at the Botanical Gardens, our first sight is reflections and reflections of reflections. Water, glass, and orchids interact causing beauty and chaos. Looking down at the water feature, the images fracture and layer until pieces become unidentifiable in a blur of colour. One step left, and things become either clearer or more muddled, depending on your starting point. One step right and the opposite happens. Only as we look up, can we see the source of the beauty—lush displays of orchids in a menagerie of shapes and colours.

We wander around, enjoying the variety of shapes and colours. I pause, sketchbook in hand, and pull out my pencils. Meanwhile, my husband raises his camera and focuses in on a flower. Each of us, in our own way, attempts to capture pieces of the beauty around us. Sketches and photos will later serve as a reference as I attempt to recreate this scene. Paint, ink, and words will become tools as I reflect and remember.

My garden pales in comparison to the lush displays at the Botanical Garden. Every summer I sink my hands into the dirt. I pull weeds. I move plants that have outgrown their spot. I trim dead branches and add support to stems bending under the weight of their flowers. Then, once again, I pull out my sketchbook to enjoy the beauty around me. I pause and let the peace of the day calm my mind.

Similarly, our lives are reflections of what we are created to be. The beauty of creation is marred by consequences of sin and selfish ambition. Gossip, grumbling, envy, and every kind of selfish action create fractures and layers which obscure the source. Look one way and pieces of healing through grace and mercy that rebuild broken relationships are visible. Beauty is being restored over layers of the past. Broken dreams are recreated in beautiful abundance through our Saviour's love and sacrifice. Look the other way and fractured lives, wounded by abuse, by fighting, and by misunderstandings left to fester and grow, leading to communities torn apart, fade into chaos.

Only hints of the beauty within remain. Only when we look up to the source do we begin to understand the incredible beauty God intended for His creation. A beauty He placed us in and invited us to enjoy. A beauty He is actively restoring for us and those around us.

My creativity, whether in the garden, my sketchbook, or my writer's notebook, is a gift from God. It, like my drawing, is a partial rendering of the source. As I study the flower and learn its characteristics, my image more accurately reflects the nature of the flower. As I dwell in the presence of God, He reveals His characteristics and infuses my life with them. I begin to reflect His peace no matter what turmoil surrounds me. As I create, I slow down, calming the chaos of thoughts and allowing myself to face whatever is happening. God, the Master Creator, leaves His mark on me just as He has done with all of creation.

GARDEN CHAOS

JEANELLE DERRY

Sunflower in floral arrangement by Ruth L. Snyder

When I am afraid, I put my trust in you. In God, whose word I praise—in God I trust and am not afraid. What can mere mortals do to me? (Psalm 56:3-4)

On a beautiful, warm, and sunny June day, my first ever sunflowers were growing nicely—with great curb appeal. I looked forward to driving past them. When I drove onto our driveway, I gave a sharp intake of breath. Neighbours had advised me that they chased a cow out of my garden in the past. The nerve in my neck twitched. Now a very large animal was trampling through my early summer garden, waving its head back and forth, chomping at my carrots and beets!

My creative haven, where I could escape the rest of the world, was being invaded. I came in hot.

The animal smelled like decaying flesh, slinging drool all over my vegetables, leaving deep hoofprints in my hard-earned, tilled dirt. I detected a unique chemical odor—my fear. After a closer look, I saw my invader was not a cow but a bull. That instantly took me back to my days of cow herding and how afraid I was of my dad's bull. With my finger on the panic button, my breathing grew shallow. I felt afraid and vulnerable.

I ran through all the mindset affirmations from the podcasts I listened to. *I can do hard things. I got this. Stay calm.* That gave me something: Nerve.

I said aloud, "Okay, Jeanelle, this is not a worst-case scenario." It was, after all, only a small setback in the big scheme of life. I approached him, grabbing the nearest thing to me, my rake and garden hoe. Maybe I could scare him more then he scared me. That's been a go-to strategy I have used my whole life. Get them before they get me.

The nerve! I thought, *Oh no, you don't! This garden is my Eden, and I am going to banish you from it!*

Moving closer to the bull, I clapped the weapons gently together. Knowing a soft tone was persuasive, I turned on the charm saying, "Come on buddy, off you go. Go Home!"

The bull turned towards me as he moved off. I saw his eyes were infected, so he was reacting blindly. That gave me some hope. It also gave me empathy. But hold on; disaster had not been averted yet. He walked away, giving me the side-eye; then he suddenly stopped, shimmied his butt quickly to one side, and swung his horned head over to take an aggressive stance in front of me. It was a quick, decisive move and very scary. I was horribly exposed. Images of what "could be" flashed through my mind.

Resisting the desire to flee, I hit the rake and hoe together again, tentatively moving forward. The noise must have irritated Mr. Bull, who turned and walked quickly out of my garden onto the driveway.

I jumped into my car for protection. A horn punched into the side of my car was better than a horn punched into the side of me. I honked the car horn near his heels, feeling more in control of my emotions. He moved purposefully to his own yard. It surprised me how well a blind bull could find his own way home!

Physically exposed to the animal's raw power was terrifying in that moment. My gut told me to remain calm. Intellectually, I have found that fighting my fear is counterproductive. Fear and vulnerability are my superpowers, are they not? They are necessary to achieve everything that I do. I use them to make quick rational decisions under pressure, using knowledge and experience from my past. Having my guard down motivates me to find an outside source of strength, the Lord. My fear becomes my strength with a daily deepening, growing relationship with Christ. When I fight fear, I focus on fear and not on Christ. I want to trust Christ, let my guard down and allow Him to take charge.

"Dear Lord, thank you for showing me I can trust You in spite of my fear. I want to practice turning to You and thinking about You, setting my eyes on things that are bigger than my circumstances. I will praise You for Your great faithfulness."

Just like I can trust my early summer garden to recover, change, and grow with no limit, I can also trust God to strengthen me despite the unpredictable and chaotic world around me.

MIDNIGHT PRAISES

RUTH L. SNYDER

And at midnight Paul and Silas prayed, and sang praises unto God: and the prisoners heard them (Acts 16:25 KJV).

It had been a long day, and I was exhausted. However, Joe[1] declared, "I'm not tired. I'm staying up all night."

I sighed as I went and read with my daughter. Sometimes Joe calmed down when I left him alone for a while. It seemed to work. I had just drifted off to sleep when a noise woke me. Joe was up. He went to the bathroom and then refused to go back to bed.

Joe struggles with mental health, and his coping skills seemed to be deteriorating. We chatted in the hallway for a couple of hours, and then he told me, "I don't need this family anymore. I'm moving to St. Paul. Tonight."

"Where will you sleep?"

"In an alley!" He went and packed his most precious possession, his laptop.

It was 2 AM. I wracked my brain, praying for wisdom. "Would you like me to take you to St. Paul to see a doctor?"

"Sure!"

A few minutes later, Joe sat beside me, chatting as I drove. At the hospital, the doctor admitted Joe and gave him medication to help him sleep. She asked me to return in the morning when a psychiatrist would assess him.

On the way home, tears filled my eyes. "Lord, why does Joe have to struggle so much?"

"Do you trust Me?"

"Yes!"

"Will you sing?"

"Now? In the dark?"

Although I like to sing, I did not feel like singing. However, I took a deep breath and sang with a shaky voice, "Jesus, Jesus, oh Jesus . . . ." None of the outward circumstances changed, but peace filled my heart.

I thought of Paul and Silas and their midnight chorus. I pondered how difficult it must have been for them to sing. I also remembered that Hebrews 13:15 urges us to " . . . offer the sacrifice of praise to God." As I continued to sing, I sensed God smiling with pleasure, not because I was struggling, but because I was choosing to trust Him as I offered up my songs of praise.

Praising God is good for our physical, mental, and emotional health. According to Healthline, "Decades of research has shown that singing individually and in groups is good for you on many levels."[2] They list these benefits of singing:

- Singing relieves stress by reducing cortisol.

- Singing boosts your immune system by increasing immunoglobulin A.
- Singing helps release hormones which increase your pain threshold.
- Singing can improve your breathing and may help prevent snoring.
- Singing strengthens your respiratory muscles and increases oxygen saturation in your blood.
- Singing often brings back forgotten memories for people struggling with dementia.
- Singing may improve your mood.
- Singing helps those with autism, Parkinson's disease, and stuttering improve their speaking ability.

I do not know what you are experiencing today, but God does. He sees you. He understands your pain. Are you willing to praise Him just as much in your "dark" times as when your life is sunny?

PART FIVE
REFLECTIONS

Lilypad by K. Payne

CARVED BY THE CREATOR

VALERIE RONALD

A West Coast carver once gave me two spoons he fashioned from the wood of Canada's only native broadleaf evergreen, an arbutus tree. I treasured the spoons for their beautiful amber-red grain and silken texture. When I lived on the coast, I was drawn to these trees with their smooth, crimson boughs and aromatic berries. The artist told me the best carving material comes from the most rugged arbutus trees because they create the densest wood in their fight to survive harsh coastal conditions. Carvers seek after the wood of a dying arbutus tree where the main trunk has split to expose the heartwood center, rich in variegated red and gold grains.

The carved spoons remind me of the work God is doing in me. It takes refining to shape this willful heart of mine into a beautiful, useful tool for the King. Arbutus trees grow in wild, twisted shapes and are not easily cultivated in other habitats. So was my heart before God tempered it by His Spirit—bent toward sin and selfish desires, not easily tamed to obey.

I grew up in the habitat of a dysfunctional family damaged by the alcohol addiction of my father. His drive to drink and pursue his career took precedence over his family. Disappointed longing for the love of my father sent me looking for acceptance in romantic relationships, even though I knew better.

In my teens, I had encountered the love of Jesus, genuinely opening my heart to Him. Yet, like a seedling trying to grow on rocky ground, my weak faith soon withered. Rather than listening to His loving voice, I let selfish desires take root.

Eventually, I found myself trapped in a marriage to an emotionally abusive man with three small children to care for and no escape in sight. I felt as if I were dying, my life split by suffering and my raw heart exposed by trauma and neglect. God sought me in that wild state, knowing the most useful creations are often shaped from a splintered heart. I gave up my selfish will, surrendering my cracked and broken life to Him. Like a woodcarver seeing potential in a dying tree, God began to shape me into something beautiful for His kingdom.

Tucked away in the book of Nehemiah is a short phrase with immense impact. When the exiled Israelites returned to rebuild the walls of Jerusalem, they discovered the Law of Moses excluded foreigners from their midst who mistreated the Israelites and called on their pagan gods to curse them. Nehemiah makes the comment, “Our God, however, turned the curse into a blessing” (Nehemiah 13:2).

That phrase lodged in my mind and spirit. Through Christ, God turned the curse of death into a blessing for believers. Physical death leads to eternal life with Him. I also experience death to self as I surrender to Christ. I no longer rule my life—my Saviour, Jesus, does. I am being reshaped into a blessing to honour Him. But it does not happen overnight or without pain.

In a broken, dying arbutus tree, a carver sees potential for beauty and usefulness. First, he must harvest the rough wood and cut it to a workable size. Then he studies the grain, determines the density, and looks for unique qualities in the wood before carving begins. The carver who made my spoons says each piece of arbutus wood is a mystery. When he first cuts into it, he always wonders what colors, patterns, and textures he will discover inside.

My potential beauty and usefulness were not a mystery to God. He knew exactly how to cut, carve, sand, and smooth to turn me into an instrument fit for use in His kingdom. The end of my marriage cut away years of infidelity and abuse inflicted by my husband, removing me from the rotting core of a dying relationship. God met me in my place of need, helping me find "hidden treasures, riches stored in secret places" (Isaiah 45:3) where I grew to know Him in a deeper, more intimate way.

I had lost my marriage, my health, my home, and my income. My young adult children struggled with the break-up of our family, yet there was little I could do to ease their pain. I recall desperately calling out to God. His carving knife cut deep into the very core of my being, yet He never abandoned me. Instead, He drew closer, reassuring me that pruning was part of the process to ground me deeper in Him. He was my heartwood. Like the central, supporting pillar of an arbutus tree gives it strength to resist severe weather conditions, allowing it to increase in size, God gave me inner strength to resist the forces coming against me so I could grow.

Gradually, a new creation took shape in God's skillful hands. Rough patches and splinters caused by years of emotional abuse began to heal, smoothed and renewed for His purposes. He used tools like His Word, prayer, and worship, so I could grow and learn.

He brought fellow believers and survivors into my life to encourage and help, giving me hope through the example of their own healed lives. Most significantly, I no longer sought affirmation from an abusive man but found my value in how God cared for me as His beloved child.

My Creator saw me as a woman shaped by adversity. He studied my grain and texture made by those adversities and chose to use me. Eventually, He re-purposed me to be a partner in church ministry with His choice of a new husband and gave me opportunities to use my writing and speaking gifts to encourage others, especially women experiencing abusive marriages. I love serving God in this way, using what I have learned through my own trials to help others.

When the carver made my arbutus spoons, he followed the unique grains and distinctive knots in each piece of wood. He knew that cutting against the grain would result in damage, making the carving useless. By carefully studying the wood, he became familiar with its traits before making the first cut.

I am thankful God knows my grain—my unique formation created by Him. He knows how I am shaped and guides me in the specific purposes He has ordained for me. My desire is to be fashioned after my arbutus spoons, beautiful and useful to God.

A KALEIDOSCOPE OF CREATIVITY

BRENDA LEYLAND

Who could even think about artistic pursuits at such a time? All thought of creativity vanished as we heard alarming news of an unknown virus fast-tracking its way across the continents. Seismic shockwaves threatened the fabric of our societies, our homes, and our very lives. Described as the greatest peacetime crisis of our lifetime, millions faced devastation. We stayed glued to our televisions, smartphones, and computers, desperate to learn what this hellish thing was.

At home, our personal world shrank—it came to a standstill. My husband and I, both retired, quarantined inside our own four walls, minds whirling with how to figure out what it meant to go out *only* for essentials, to mask up, social distance, and stick to one's cohort group. All to stay safe in a world that felt unsafe and scary. It didn't seem quite appropriate to carry on with business as usual; for many, there was no business to carry on with. For me, I asked myself how I could continue writing on my blog about living a beautiful life amid such circumstances.

Tulips by Brenda Leyland

Still, hope is that feathered thing that rises on a breath of air. And glimpses of it began shimmering out of the darkness. In our home, it happened to be the spring bulbs we planted in pots months earlier. No one could have imagined just how priceless those little brown globes of promise would become. The world had shut down around us, but inside our house it was a veritable greenhouse of bulbs sprouting and blooming in shades of spring daffodils, tulips, hyacinth, and irises. My troubled thoughts lightened. My camera took on new significance as it captured shades of beauty from every angle at every stage. Those harbingers of spring soon appeared on my blog and social media, their message to the world: *Look at us. Take hope, dear friends, take hope.*

Still super-glued to my smartphone for the latest news, there was something else going on out there, something most interesting. People were converging on social media platforms like I'd never seen before. Creatives began saying, "We can't do our normal things; we're stuck in our homes. What can we do to keep occupied and sane? How can we support each other during these ghastly days?"

Creativity and creative expression blossomed and exploded. Artists, writers, and performers took to social media, creating community despite the isolation. Opera divas sang from their balconies. Pianists performed spontaneous concerts in their homes. Artists painted. One actor began reciting Shakespeare's sonnets—all 154 of them in as many days. And actor, Jennifer Ehle, with her oh-so-familiar Elizabeth Bennet voice (1995 film), started reading *Pride and Prejudice* to the delight of her followers on Instagram.

Artistic energy radiated through cyberspace. And to our huge surprise, people everywhere were joining in. Children hung their art from their living room windows. Folks stocked up on flour and yeast, turning their kitchens into centres of doughy creativity. People offered their "regular life" skills on YouTube videos and showed us how to exercise in place, cut our own hair, play the guitar, paint, and quilt. You name it, they showed us how to create it at home. At first, I was content enough to be an observer appreciating their many efforts. Soon I longed to join in—I wanted to be a part of this astounding phenomenon. Pandemic or not, my heart still pulsed with the desire to write about life's beautiful moments. People more than ever needed some respite, a few moments that made them feel normal in an abnormal time. I wanted to offer them something that buoyed the spirits and provided a hint of beauty so that, once heartened, they could carry on.

So, what could I offer? Well, I could blog more often, every day for a season, instead of weekly. I had books. I could press my books into service and write about my favourites. You know how it is when you visit friends in their homes; you hanker to peek at their bookshelves. Since readers couldn't come to my house, I brought the books to my readers. I chose volumes that would inspire, give comfort, and provide a sense of well-being. It was especially meaningful to find comments from readers who were so glad I was still there, writing, despite the strange times. My purpose was confirmed. The horrid sense of isolation faded. I felt connected—my online community was real. Something lovely and unexpected came out of this book series. The author of a favourite book I had written about got in touch with me all the way from The Netherlands. Daniel Blajan had authored a delightful volume twenty-five years earlier, and during COVID-19 lockdowns, he found my blog post about it and emailed me. We enjoyed a small flurry of emails back and forth across the Atlantic, and then one day his charming real mail letter arrived in the post with a personalized autograph. It's now safely tucked inside my copy of *Foxgloves & Hedgehog Days: Secrets in a Country Garden.*

Summer came and our flower garden, like the tulips earlier, gave us infinite joy and beauty during those stay-at-home days. My iPhone camera captured hundreds of floral poses, and soon many of them were being published on my blog and social media. I designed several photo books, including one that featured my mom's gorgeous Peace Rose, which I gave to her on her socially distanced 85th birthday. Another album, also for my mom, showcased her family, including pets, scattered across the provinces, to document our COVID-19-restricted first year. It included visits out in parking lots, family birthday cakes enjoyed virtually, and happy but heart-sad pictures of my dear niece's wedding, which her entire family could attend only via Zoom.

Home, usually a peaceful place, became a true sanctuary. I no longer felt the restrictions as I had at first. I found purpose and, despite all, continued to catch glimpses of heaven in unexpected places, right in my own house and neighbourhood. The simpler, slower pace of my days gave me other opportunities to be more reflective. I engaged in several smaller creative pursuits, such as sorting through old scrapbooks from my school days and writing some of those stories that still wanted to be told. I picked up my love of writing old-fashioned letters the snail-mail way and stocked up on boxes of artsy greeting cards (thanks to Amazon's delivery service). Along with my handwritten notes, I'd tuck in small surprises: sachets of tea, quotes, stickers, blank postcards, anything fun that snugged inside a card-size envelope. The real thrill for me was imagining a friend's face when she discovered real mail waiting for her in the mailbox.

Out of these tumultuous times came beautiful things. My mind, a creative blank, having gone into hiding at the outset, was set free when I poured myself into something other than fretfulness and anxiety. The kaleidoscope of quiet creativity, in a variety of shapes, colours, and focuses, buoyed my spirits and kept me sane. My hands kept busy, and my mind stayed on Him. I will never forget the world's ingenious creative response to this terrible season. And I am so grateful to have been a tiny part of this luminous worldwide creativity during a global pandemic.

Words of Gold

PHIL CALLAWAY

We sometimes use the wrong words in conversations. Just ask the husband who said, "Having one wife is called monotony." I assume he meant "monogamy." When I was a kid, I told my mom a friend got *exploded* from school. She was surprised. "That's a little harsh," she said.

Such mix-ups are called malapropisms, the misuse of similar-sounding words. This word confusion leads to some unintentional linguistic creativity, which can bring a delightfully humorous outcome.

For instance, here are classic examples of word blunders from kids. "I helped my dad in the garage. He let me hit some nails in with his *hamster*." Ouch. Poor hamster. That's not a nice way to go. A proud niece said, "Auntie Mary will be having a baby in March because she is *stagnant*."

Kids also learn some interesting things in school that will tickle your funny bone. Like this: "In Geography we learned that countries with a sea round them are islands and ones without a sea are *incontinents*."

This is from an essay, "In wartime, it was safer in the country. Children who lived in big cities had to be *evaporated*." An 8-year-old had this to say about composition: "When you are writing, if you don't want to use a full stop on a sentence, you can use an *excitement* mark instead."

Kids get their merds wixed up, and it's always fun to be around when it happens. "When you write a story," said one, "you should do a *daft* copy first. Then you can change it round and make it sound better." I've written a few daft copies myself, inadvertently. But, more often, I write about humorous moments to lift readers' spirits and help them cope with life's troublesome times.

Equally entertaining are children's perspectives of everyday life. They are frequently found guilty of sharing "TMI" (too much information). A little girl said, "My uncle shouts at my cousins and makes them do chores. One day they are going to be policemen and policewomen so they can put him in prison."

Another little girl said, "I sleep in my bedroom. My brother sleeps in his bedroom. My mummy sleeps in hers and daddy's bedroom, but daddy sometimes sleeps on the sofa with our dog. I think this is because he growls like a dog when he is snoring in his sleep."

An adult asked a little boy whose mother was expecting, "Do you want a boy or a girl?" The boy attempted to parrot his parents and said, "We don't care if it's a boy or a girl, just as long as it's *wealthy*."

I am also guilty of accidently inserting incorrect words and thoughts into conversations. Sometimes this word confusion is funny. Sometimes it's belittling or demeaning. One of my prayers, lately, is that God would help me use words that build something positive and noble.

Proverbs 25:11 (NRSV) says, "A word fitly spoken is like apples of gold in a setting of silver." The right word at just the right time is a work of art. Just ask Mary. She always knew she was different from the other kids, and she hated it. Hated their teasing about her physical features. Hated being different. Hated that she could barely hear with one ear. Then she entered Mrs. Leonard's class. Her teacher was kind and gracious; she smiled a lot. This was the 1950s and teachers routinely administered an annual hearing test. During that test, Mrs. Leonard whispered softy into Mary's deaf ear while Mary pretended to plug her good ear. The teacher whispered seven words that Mary heard clearly. Words she held onto. Words that changed her life. For Mary, these "[words] fitly spoken [were] like apples of gold in a setting of silver."

We, too, can deliberately choose to use precious words of gold to affirm and uplift others: "Way to go." "Thanks for your friendship." "If I knew it would be this good, I'd have married you in grade eight." "You brighten a room." They may be exactly what someone needs to hear, and they could be life changing.

The words Mrs. Leonard spoke? "I wish you were my little girl."

THE REDEMPTION OF A TEXT MESSAGE

MICHELLE STRUTZENBERGER

I learned about my mom's death from a text. Like black splinters, the teeny print on my phone screen proclaimed the end of one of the most precious people in my life.

I had been expecting the news and wasn't surprised it came the way it did. It was spring 2020. The world had just been shuttered by the pandemic. While in any other time my siblings and I would have flown immediately to be with Mom in her final days, it was exactly that period when jets had been grounded and flights indefinitely put on hold.

For weeks, we had been receiving text updates from my sister Carolyn on my 88-year-old mom's diminishing health. With eight siblings living in three Canadian provinces, one state in the USA, and the Central American country of Belize, we had agreed to relieve the communication burden on my sister and join a group chat. Carolyn was already going through the most as the daughter who lived closest to my mom in Belize.

It was painful not to be near my mother in her time of greatest weakness and vulnerability—the woman who had been near me, a gentle and reassuring presence in my worst moments as a preteen blindsided by culture shock after our move to Canada and, later, as a young adult shattered by the death of my twin. In both those times, my mom would have been struggling with her own adjustments and grief, but she never stopped showing up.

Every morning, she rose, brushed her hair, and slipped on a clean blouse and pants. Then she'd quietly putter in the kitchen, stirring up aromas of coffee and toast. I would find her reading devotions in the living room. I'd see her leaving the house, sitting beside my dad in the pick-up truck as they ran errands together.

Never, until now, have I understood how much those simple, non-dramatic acts of hers would help me cope. I realize now they were some of her greatest gifts to me.

My mom did so much for me all my life, but I couldn't show up for her in her final days. I was thankful, of course, that she had my sister, who spent hours at her bedside, holding mom's now terribly thin hands, repeatedly singing her favourite hymns in a hushed voice. Two of my brothers also lived in the area and visited often.

My mom died just before dawn in the long-term care home in Belize. A few hours before, thousands of miles away in Ontario, Canada, I suddenly awoke. As I lay in the dark, I wondered if my mom's spirit was leaving this earth.

In the morning, the phone screen was splintered with the sharp message.

Our family has experienced the deaths of several of our close loved ones over the years—my twin, my oldest sister, my dad, and my nephew. Every time, the grief mashes the spirit. But in all those moments, we as a family could come together. Our spirits could draw strength from our physical bodies sharing the same space, looking into one another's tear-wet faces, grabbing one another's hands, clutching each other in fierce hugs.

This time, we couldn't have that. Stuck in my pandemic-forced isolation, I would be grieving my precious mom without the comfort of my siblings.

I remember the day my mom died as being overcast—a dull sky, the air still, not a single bird or cricket sound.

And then a new text message unfurled across my screen from my brother in Belize. They were planning to bury my mom the same day with a small service on the hill. Would I be willing to write her eulogy that day?

My family of seven living siblings could have picked anyone to write my mom's eulogy. They picked me, the youngest. They all know I write as a hobby, and it's quite likely that's the main reason they asked me. But I believe the Holy Spirit might have moved them as well. He knew just what I needed to help me get through that day.

I spun a text back to my brother exclaiming, "Yes, please! Of course, I would love to." Then I hunkered down at the end of the dining room table, clutching a pen over a stack of lined paper, a glass of water at my elbow. My spirit and thoughts strained towards realizing this new aspiration as I earnestly set about to do my very best work.

As I stitched in mom's birth date, my imagination swung back to her beginnings, long before my birth. I remembered the stories she'd told us of growing up on the shores of Lake Erie in a brick farmhouse with five sisters and four brothers. My heart ached as I felt the breezy sunshine off the shore and heard the children's laughter and singing of long ago. I couldn't write all the stories in her eulogy, but they came crowding round my spirit, skimming off a sweet longing.

I did add a line about her choice as an eight-year-old to follow Jesus.

As I wove in her wedding date, her years of raising children on a farm and then travelling as a missionary family for decades unrolled around me. Again, I felt a strange anguish in my heart as I saw her watching over her young children while they played.

The hours in the silent dining room tiptoed by as memories flocked round. I tried to yank them down onto my page just right, in a way that did them justice; that did my precious mom's life justice.

Of course, in the end, I was not completely satisfied. Pausing for a swish of water while I reread my work, I noticed the messy sentences and not-quite-perfectly-placed words. I tried to straighten up my writing, quickly swiping at that smudge of a wrongly placed verb, smoothing down that stray not-quite-right adjective.

But my family was ready for the eulogy. I had to send it.

With the tap of my computer mouse, the Word document appeared on my brother's phone in Belize.

My siblings streamed the funeral over Facebook so that those of us who couldn't be there physically could join with our eyes and ears.

The wind from thousands of miles away thumped at the camera's microphone, snatching away words and parts of songs as the minister and my siblings and their children held the funeral service for my mom on a sunny hill. The sky behind them rose a white blue.

A granddaughter, Amy, played on a keyboard teetering on the dry, rocky ground beside the grave. The music felt like a cool cloth on a fevered head.

And then it was time for the eulogy to be read. "Michelle wrote this today," my brother said, before starting to read. The wind pulled away many of the sentences from his mouth even while it flapped the paper and rustled his hair.

After that, the grandchildren, young men, carried my mother's casket to the graveside and slowly lowered it. It was when I heard the first shovel of dirt hit the wooden top that I cried. Dirt thudding on a coffin proclaims, "This is the end."

I hadn't cried all day.

All day, I had been swathed in memory and creating, in love and hope. Writing my mom's eulogy had given that to me, and I was so deeply grateful, especially since I couldn't be with my family.

You could say this was one way the harsh morning text message had been redeemed.

But there was another way.

What was the most important line I had written in my mom's eulogy? She asked Jesus into her heart.

Because of that line, because of the choice she had made as a little girl, I could cry, I could miss her, and I could mourn that I wasn't grieving with my siblings, but *not as one without hope*. I could say, as millions of Christians have said before me, "Where, O death, is your victory? Where, O death, is your sting?"(1 Corinthians 15:55).

The splintery text message I had received that morning had proclaimed: "Mom's gone."

But the message I sent back at the end of the day, at the very end of the eulogy I had written, exulted in the words of a poem my dad had written long before:

"The trials at last all are ended

The service on Earth here is done

Victorious with all of God's people

Eternity's blessings begun!"

A fact had flown across the cellphone networks that morning, splintering our hearts.

But Truth raced back across the world that evening, slowly starting the process of stitching them back together.

The Art of Facing Chaos

PAT GERBRANDT

If anyone knew about chaos, it was Tevye in *Fiddler on the Roof*. As I consider the things that trouble me, I also realize I can glean lessons from that factitious dairy farmer. Tevye philosophizes his way through chaotic happenings and relies on music to help him along the way.

Chaos, or inner turmoil, has simmered in my subconscious ever since family stress erupted. Despite my attempts at reconciliation and prayers for all concerned, the situation is unchanged. One person's choices and experiences spread to become a painful reality for others.

I once heard a grown man talk about his mother's strange melancholy at certain times of the year. He noted how she often seemed distant, not only at Christmas or other times of celebration, but also during times that had no significance to anyone else in the family. Then the woman's firstborn child, a girl she'd given up for adoption at birth, contacted her. The man went on to thank his new-found sister for diligence in searching for her birth parent. "We have our mom back, and a bonus sister, too." A long-held secret was revealed, and the mother no longer mourned when her firstborn's birthday came around.

I understand a little of the melancholy associated with special events because the absence of loved ones is accentuated at those times. For too long, I didn't recognize what was happening and could find no tangible way to express my unidentified longings.

Shortly before pandemic restrictions affected all of us, I'd begun learning stamping and card-making. When it was impossible to buy greeting cards, I realized the tools for my new hobby would allow me to send cards offering cheer to others.

Convinced that celebrating a person's birthday is an affirmation of personal worth, I vowed to keep making birthday cards for our estranged loved ones just as I do for others. Working with colour and design, composing a card especially for each recipient helps me to channel energy that might otherwise be expended in useless fretting. I pray for the person as I select a theme, arrange the elements of each card, and then relinquish the finished product to the care of postal services.

I confess card-making is more craft than art, but working with colour, design, and composition is satisfying. The simple tools—stamps and dies—are easy enough to use so that I can achieve reasonably good results. I hope that every card will serve as a quiet messenger of love. Many beautiful, tasteful greeting cards are available for purchase, but making my own requires time and mindfulness, and impels me to invest my "work" for the sake of each recipient.

Since the cards I make generally carry few words, I also need to write. Sometimes a great torrent of words fills the pages. When I began writing, I was content to find just the right words and to use them correctly. Sentence structure fascinates me. There's a satisfying orderliness to correct grammar, and there is also the exquisite delight of using words correctly and, sometimes, in surprising ways. But, unique or not, working with words for the sake of using words is mechanical.

Stanley Fish maintains " . . . just piling up words, one after the other, won't do much of anything until something else has been added."[1] He turns to Anthony Burgess for this revelation:

> *And the words slide into the slots ordained by syntax,*
> *And glitter as with atmospheric dust with those impunities*
> *Which we call meaning.*[2]

Writing helps me to organize my thoughts. I strive for logical order of those ideas. I need to make sure my sentences are constructed so they say what I intend them to say. Sometimes, seeing what I have written helps me determine whether the piece is worth sharing. Do I really want to share these thoughts? Do I need to? By writing, I put chaotic emotions "in their place" on paper or a computer screen, then determine how to continue.

Learning how to develop a piece of writing seems to parallel a progression in the ability to analyze situations. This has surprised me greatly. Growing up an only child, I often felt dwarfed by the adults in my life. In my later teens, I still felt like a child intellectually among more mature people. I was aware of my inability to think objectively. I nearly despaired of ever having discernment. Feeling devoid of any sense of logic troubled me.

Since then, learning to rework a piece of writing to achieve greater clarity has helped me ask big questions about bigger issues. Working in the constituency office for two consecutive Members of the Legislature for several years, I never knew what kind of chaotic situation might be presented. There I had to learn discernment and find ways of communicating that were most effective. My responsibilities did not call for "making things happen," so carefully chosen words were essential. I am grateful God increased my ability to think on my feet and that He continues to give me greater understanding of things happening around me.

I will never fully understand the chaos that I experience or all the turmoil that occurs in the world. All I can do is face life realistically and with a courage that comes from God. I can convey caring by writing and with cards. Most of all, I want to communicate God's gift of grace to a hurting world. With writing, as with card making, I want to be sensitive to God's ways. The Psalmist's prayer is mine, "Search me, O God, and know my heart! Try me and know my thoughts! And see if there be any grievous way in me, and lead me in the way everlasting!" (Psalm 139:23, 24 ESV).

Then I can get to work, keeping in mind Proverbs 16:3, "Commit your work to the Lord, and your plans will be established."

Chaos likely will not end. Like Tevye in *Fiddler on the Roof*, I try to make sense of my world and use card making and writing in the process. Tevye relies on different forms of art as he tries to make sense of the chaos erupting all around him. His philosophizing is like an oral form of essay writing, his sense of humour is therapeutic, and throughout the entire production, the dairy farmer's poetic expressions take shape in song.

Perhaps there's a bit of Tevye in many of us.

DISCOVERY

LORILEE GUENTER

I hold my pen poised above the paper with trepidation. Words and emotions collide in a dizzying array, waiting to be loosed, shaped, moulded. The chaos of thoughts obscures details, becoming a place to retreat into noise, unwilling or unable to escape the turmoil. News headlines compete with daily activity, with plans for visiting friends and family, and with plans for rest. He said this, she said that; they are certain, but no one knows for sure. The noise continues, swirling into chaos and potential confusion. Sides are taken; relationships are strained.

I place my pen to the paper. A stroke here, an arc there, words and images emerge. Some are coherent. Others await clarification. The thoughts, though jumbled, instruct. They encourage me to make the first step. One word becomes two. Sentence builds on sentence. I see my thoughts in black and white and begin to understand. My place is here and now, with family and friends. We do not need to know everything. I can add to the chaos, or I can pause, reflect, and begin to build bridges. I can rest in the fact that God is still in control.

My characters form and grow as they experience place and time. They allow me to consider *what if* and *what then* as they face fear and uncertainty or joy and celebration. The causes are many, each unique and yet the same. Is the character me or a piece of my imagination? It could be both. After all, I am the creator. My curiosity and questions inform each word scribbled across the page.

"I did not expect that!" is spoken as the characters come to life before me. It is another form of "Aha!" I never would have thought of that if I had not played with the chaos simmering just beyond my consciousness. The pen brought the ideas forward, allowing excavation and exploration. My characters act and react in their own ways to mental health struggles, to abuse, to illness and loss. They connect with community and celebrate each step of healing, of friendship, and of grace. Others withdraw, floundering on their own, either unwilling or unable to let go of the pain for even one moment. Some of these struggles I have experienced; others I witnessed in friends as I walked beside them. On my own, I am helpless to understand, to act. I process on the page as I pray.

My mind settles into a rhythm of discovery as I analyze the world around me through the tip of my pen. I wander into poetry, inviting the reader to engage as a character dropped into images. I invite exploration, appreciation, or wrestling as I have done. Perhaps my words propel them in a different direction, or perhaps not. The path may twist and turn. Roadblocks here, discoveries there, and I cannot see the end from the beginning. I do not need to. It will come in its own time, arriving when the chaos turns to calm. The pen has explained events, identified emotions, and informed actions. Perhaps that is why the pen is mightier than the sword. It has the power to build and explain. The sword can only defend and destroy.

I pick up my pen with anticipation as I await the discoveries of today. I set it to paper and watch thoughts unfold as they come to order. I explore new questions and curiosities. Today is less chaotic; tomorrow might be worse. In either case, God will meet me on the page. He knows what I need.

THE EPIPHANY

JANEY BORDIHN

The other day, I had an epiphany. It wasn't earth shattering, but it was meaningful to me. I was listening to music when an old song came on, and I began to sing along. I'm always amazed that after the first chord of a familiar song is played, the lyrics jump from the recesses of memory to my tongue, enabling me to sing the entire song. Many times, I haven't heard the song for decades or don't even realize that I know it! And just as the melody and lyrics of the song are such a part of me, so is the meaning I have ascribed to it. They are my interpretations, and every time I hear the song, they are affirmed.

Except not so much anymore. I've changed. Life experience has expanded my narrow vision and rooted out the arrogant judgement of youth. Life is clearly not as black and white as I thought it was in my twenties. In fact, now it seems the whole landscape is gray. Black and white is non-existent or increasingly difficult to find.

So, as I sang one line of this particular song, I understood it in a completely different way. This revelation really struck me. As I turned this epiphany over in my mind, examining and expanding on it, I began to craft sentences and explanations, for—of course—I was going to write this down. It was brilliant! OK, maybe it wasn't brilliant and would fall flat on the page and never go out for the masses to read. But it was interesting to me, and I was running with it. Who knows what it might become? Then, in my hubris, I did it again. I had an idea, crafted eloquent prose, and committed it to memory.

Why, oh why can't I learn that my memory is not to be trusted? It's flighty, finicky, unreliable—a trickster. Now, my trusty pen is always ready for me, and its ink does not disappear. I should have written it down. What a shameful word, "should"! But this idea was so good, so deep, that I thought I couldn't possibly forget it. And I won't even tell you how many times this has happened to me, lest my shiny image dulls right before your eyes. On many occasions, I have ignored my thoughts or shelved them for later and turned my eyes back to the demands of my life, only to have their tyrannical clamour crowd the thoughts right out of my mind. Was I waiting for a better time? I should (there is that word again!) know that if I wait until I have time, or my life is in a better place, or I am in a different frame of mind, it will probably be a long time away. I can't remember what meal I ate earlier, so why would I expect to remember my thoughts after a length of time?

Now, I am taunted by my memory. Illusive wisps of sentence fragments hover and dance at the edges of my brain, only to fly away as I strain to grasp them. I try to remember and recreate. I check my recent playlists—just waiting for a band name, song title, or idea to resurface. I alternately berate and meditate. I try to conjure up something akin to that song's first chord to have my thoughts come flooding back to me. But so far? Nothing. Still no epiphany to share.

Exactly what was I doing that was so urgent? I know better than to believe all the tasks of my day are more important. I know I must not let anything stop me from jotting down a few thoughts. I thought I would never forget the insights I gained from our recent pandemic!

When all else was stripped away, I realized how vital writing was to me. Taking my ideas, situations, and the emotions I'm feeling and translating them into words is not only cathartic for me, but it also provides a filter of sorts. Creating sentences forces me to step back a bit and often I gain some needed perspective, even in the midst of big emotions or global crisis. I also learned I had to turn off the television and my phone because I did not want the incessant loud voices of media to consume my thoughts with the world's latest scares and impending catastrophes and drown out my own voice.

Reinforced to me during those years of our global pandemic was the truth that we are much more than flesh and bones. We are heart, soul, mind, and body. All are important and vital to our overall health. In that time of cessation of my "normal" life, I had plenty of time for introspection. I considered whether the arts were just entertainment, or distractions from life, or intrinsic to life—my life and humanity's at large. I wondered how important it was for me to write about my thoughts or situations when much bigger things were happening. But in that time, my pen and journal, books, and music were my lifelines. They filled my restless locked-in days and provided necessary nourishment to my heart and soul, along with inspiration to pick up my pen despite the hyperbole and fear of the daily news that left me feeling immobilized or anxious.

Words of truth and experiences help us to cope, understand, and most of all, they connect us. And boy, in our isolation, we soon realized how much we need connection. We need theatre, with its story, song, and dance, inviting us into lessons of history and humanity. We need artwork to notice and reflect beauty, memorializing moments. We need poetry for its lyrical wordplay, connection, raw emotion, and truth. We need the insightful lyrics and unforgettable melodies of songs that speak to our hearts and minds, adding joy to our lives. We need writers of all manner of things to be the faithful witnesses to, and communicators of, life. It is we, the creatives of the world, who can give voice to our personal situations and times. As we do, we gain greater clarity, insight, and strength to live more resiliently and help others do the same. Additionally, we, the people of faith, who have hope for the future and in God, need to continue to be a light in our world. Especially when it seems dark.

So, I understood my need to honour my urge to write things down and followed through by doing just that. Write things down! Always. I thought I had learned this well during the pandemic, but I suppose I will forever be a student who must revisit her lessons.

So, it appears that instead of sharing my latest epiphany, my newfound meaning, alas, I am only relearning and retelling an old lesson. One that is not particularly interesting or nuanced, just infuriatingly ordinary and obvious. It is very simple. Write it down! Maybe this lesson wasn't just for me, but for all who create. We who craft in our minds and then, out of laziness, busyness, procrastination, fear, undervaluation of our own work, or any myriad of excuses, fail to bring our vision to fruition. We need to remember and repeat the following four points:

1. If I have an epiphany, a vision, an observation, a story, a character, a melody, an idea, inkling, hint, or echo—write it down.
2. Even if I don't have it all figured out or know whether it will be awe-inspiring or ordinary—write it down.
3. No matter how or what I am feeling—write it down.
4. No matter what is going on in the world, what I am doing at the moment, what circumstances are happening in my life, whether my life is going well, has stalled, upended, or is spinning out of control—write it down.

And just maybe this was what I was supposed to write all along.

FINDING HOPE

TANDY BALSON

Henry Wadsworth Longfellow once wrote, "And the cares that infest the day, / Shall fold their tents, like the Arabs, / And as silently steal away."[1] Oh, that my cares would silently steal away. But they were not easily dismissed. Although I did my best to ignore news from the world outside my safe haven, it filtered through to my consciousness. The year was 2020 and the media was full of doom and gloom. These reports only added to my negative state of mind.

We had just downsized, or rightsized, as some people call it. Our house was much larger than we needed, so the move made sense on a practical level. The emotional side of it was another matter entirely. Most decisions on what to keep and what to let go fell to me. The stress was overwhelming at times as I said goodbye to treasured mementos.

We moved into our apartment in the days when social distancing was mandatory. Everyone in the building kept to themselves, which meant there was no opportunity to meet our new neighbours. In our smaller living area, it was a challenge for my husband and me to create personal space. We had a good relationship, but the constant togetherness became a challenge for both of us. My creativity dried up. I would sit in front of the computer and stare at a blank screen, unable to write. The frustration I felt gave weight to my downward emotional spiral.

In desperation one day, I pulled out an acrylic painting kit from the back of my closet. My painting experience was minimal and only under the guidance of an experienced tutor. Daunted by the thought of doing this on my own, I remembered the encouraging words of my painting mentor: “Don’t worry about making a mistake. One of two things will happen. Either you paint over it and start again, or it becomes a happy accident.” I took courage from this and figured out how to set up the easel. Next, I found a photo reference to give me direction. After placing a clean, fresh canvas in front of me, I took a deep breath and started brushing on paint. The dark colours I used seemed appropriate for my current mindset.

This project gave me hours of enjoyment as I experimented with an ever-changing colour palette. Low expectations gave me the freedom to create without fear of failure. My finished project bore little resemblance to the reference photo, and I did not care! I was proud of myself for creating something. The sunbeams streaming through dark clouds now painted on the canvas represented HOPE to me. I named my painting *Hope* and asked my husband to hang it on my wall above my desk.

Whenever I look at it, I’m reminded of the hope that God brings. That hope has encouraged me to once again craft words on a blank page. They do not have to be perfect, and I occasionally erase what I have and start again. More often, God takes my humble beginnings and turns them into something unexpected. It is my hope that these happy accidents will provide encouragement for someone else.

Listen, can you hear it, too? It is the sound of my cares folding their tents and slipping away.

DEVELOPING A CREATIVE LIFESTYLE IN TRYING TIMES

SANDI SOMERS

When COVID-19 burst onto our world in 2020, life crumbled as if hit by a wrecking ball. Shock, anger, frustration, and fear became the norm, especially if individuals or loved ones succumbed. As I connected with others, watched TV, or listened to radio commentators, I discovered that without normal life activities, some became bored and watched Netflix or scrolled social media incessantly. Others lost their purpose and struggled with mental health issues. Some writer friends became too paralyzed to write—COVID-19 had bled their creativity. Yet others tried grappling with what the pandemic meant on a personal, local, and even worldwide level. They accepted the setbacks and adapted the best they could.

However, I noticed how the absence of normal busy lives—sometimes overly-busy—allowed people the space to discover new meaning that transcended the limitations to find new purposes.

I discovered that some people needed to re-examine false foundations on which they had built their lives. In a radio interview during the early stages of COVID-19, one man couldn't believe why he had been "going in a million directions," juggling his time between taking his children every evening to lessons and sports activities, attending after-hours work meetings, and being on the go 24/7. Realizing that he had no quality time with his family was a personal awakening which led him to begin reprioritizing his life to make it more meaningful.

I paid attention to how others explored dormant potentials and new creative ventures. Facebook friends experimented with new skills in baking, meal planning, repairing, or remodelling their homes. Others learned a new language with online classes. Once stores began opening, bicycle shops sold out of bicycles. RV sales shot up. In my own experience, when I wanted to buy a specific bird book for my great-nephew, all copies on Amazon and in bookstores were sold out.

Creativity spurred success, and the most successful were those who found unique ways to develop their own artistic expression. Industries switched normal operations to making face shields, plastic protectors, and hand sanitizers. Some with sewing abilities built a home business designing protective masks, advertising and selling them on the internet.

I watched TV documentaries of apartment dwellers in European cities, confined within the four walls of their apartments, meeting at a designated time each evening to sing and play their instruments on their balconies. This not only provided them with a creative release, but it also connected them with others. Throughout the world, choirs and orchestras developed synchronized performances using Zoom recordings. Zoom meetings and workshops/podcasts became the norm.

And then I discovered my own creativity, right on my doorstep. I wrote and then attached to my fridge Marcel Proust's wisdom: "The real voyage of discovery consists not in seeking new landscapes but in having new eyes" (La Prisonnière, 1923). When our church services were shut down, I travelled to sites in Calgary and outlying areas early Sunday mornings to reengage with birdwatching. I went on extended walks. I explored new trails around my community and beyond.

Unable to visit family members, I phoned and wrote letters to my great-nieces and great-nephews who were being home schooled. After many of these excursions and activities, I wrote articles, some of which I later published.

Beyond creative outlets spurred by COVID-19, I drew on what I had learned earlier: processing feelings through the arts is valuable in regaining and maintaining mental health.

James Pennebaker, a pioneer of writing therapy, advocated expressive writing to ease feelings of emotional distress. This takes the form of journaling frustrations, thoughts, and feelings.[1] But I found that it's necessary to write beyond just the frustrations to discover insight, meaning, and a new perspective.

Journaling became a healing process in the months leading up to my mom's passing in 2010. I had been reading through my Bible and came to the book of Job. There I journaled more than usual, writing thoughts and insights on suffering and faith. I integrated this writing with Paul's instructions on how to respond to grief and suffering. He brought new meaning to the greater purpose of our suffering, going beyond ourselves to encourage and comfort other believers and so further the cause of Christ (2 Corinthians 1:4).

Reviewing past experiences further, I had discovered through teaching my immigrants that many from non-Western countries are unaccustomed to formal "talk therapies" and are unwilling to share intimate details with a stranger. Even if they do, sometimes words could not be found to describe their traumatic experiences. Instead, they found creative release through engaging in bodily expressive arts such as drawing and drama. Bessel van der Kolk, in his book, *The Body Keeps the Score*,[2] eloquently developed the principle that overwhelming experiences affect the brain, mind, and body. Tension is stored in the body, and body arts such as dancing, singing, and acting release this tension and enhance mental health. This valuable and conscious activity is a practice which all of us would do well to remember.

All my reflections on COVID-19 and my earlier experiences have taught me that creative expression will bring wellness and value that offset the fright and frustration of trying times. It will help us view life as "full of new possibilities, discoveries, exploration, experimentation, self-expression, and invention. It's a habit, a way of being, a style of existing."[3] The more aware and prepared we are to face crises and the more we draw on God's resources, the more resilient and stronger we will become, and the more encouraging to others we will be.

PART SIX
MEMOIR

Purity of Heart by Shannon Erickson

A Light Within

BARBARA FULLER

A Light Within by Barbara Fuller

Down on her knees, five-year-old Leora pushed open the tiny door of the miniature church. She leaned over and peered through the windows at the wee pews inside. The little platform and the light inside lent an air of welcome expectation, as if a teeny pastor and his mini congregation would soon be arriving.

Leora gathered all the animals from the manger scene and lined them up outside the door of the church. "Everybody wants to go to church, Grandma," she explained. "But they couldn't go through the little door so they climbed on each other's backs so they could see inside the church too." How her grandpa Gerry would have loved that!

I smiled as I remembered Leora's mother peering through those windows when she was young. Every Christmas for more than thirty-five years, I have brought the little church down from the top shelf, dusted it off, and plugged it in as part of our Christmas decorations.

The miniature church was crafted by a man named Joe. Joe ran a taxi service in the Annapolis Valley of Nova Scotia. His British wife, Pat, worked as a care aide at a local seniors' home. A warm and nurturing couple, their son, Gary, had been best friends with my husband, Gerry, throughout their teen years. Then one day, just a few years after Gerry and I were married, Pat and Joe's world fell apart. An RCMP constable arrived at their door and notified them that their son, Gary, had been killed in a motorcycle accident. The next days were a blur of tears, questions, embraces, arrangements, and a sense of walking in a fog. Lost, clinging to one another and unable to grasp that their only son was gone.

When we heard the tragic news of Gary's death, Gerry was grief-stricken. Together we went to visit Gary's heartbroken parents. They had always treated Gerry like a son despite the shenanigans the boys got into. Gerry's home life had been marred by mental illness and emotional insecurity, but the warmth and humour in their home had provided a refuge for him. Now they were the ones who needed refuge. It had been years since they had seen each other, but Joe embraced Gerry in a bear hug and held him tightly, tears in his eyes. Pat opened her arms and warmly received my sympathetic hug, even though we had never met.

With a touch of Gerry's hand and his gentle loving gaze, the floodgates opened. Pat and Joe poured out the story of Gary's accident, the haunting questions, their grief, and the agony of parents who had lost a child. As a friend and as a pastor, Gerry listened to them, loved them, wept with them, and then said an honest prayer to the God he trusted, whom they weren't so sure about. Gerry continued to visit the family over the next days and weeks, and Joe didn't forget how this "adopted" son had helped them through their darkest days.

Sometime later, Joe heard that Gerry was pastoring his first church in a nearby community. He considered how he might express his appreciation to Gerry. Nova Scotia was dotted with small country churches, most very similar in construction and appearance. Looking around his workshop, Joe chose some pieces of wood leftover from other projects. He made some sketches, then started measuring and sawing. He started with the wooden base and began working on the interior of the model church. At the front, he made a platform with four tiny steps leading up to it. Up those steps, a Lilliputian organist might go to the miniature organ in the corner and sit on the wee bench behind it. Joe fashioned two pews for a choir, one longer against the rear wall and a shorter front pew. In the centre of the podium, he placed a pulpit. He smiled as he envisioned Gerry standing behind the pulpit in a country church much like this one. Attentive to every detail, Joe used his jigsaw to create a wooden railing for the front of the podium, designed with rounded tops and tiny drilled holes.

For the main part of the church, Joe created perfect miniature pews—five on one side and four on the other where the steps were. He stained all the petite wooden pieces with a reddish-brown stain. While they dried, he measured and cut pieces of red felt for the floor of the platform and the main part of the church. Once he glued the felt in place, then he delicately installed the stained pews, railing, organ, and pulpit. Joe was grateful to have a project like this to keep his hands and mind busy. It made him feel hopeful.

As he installed a wee door at the entry of the tiny replica, he thought of the day when he and Pat might go and hear Gerry preach at his real church. Once the interior was complete, Joe worked on the outside pieces. He carefully cut the window openings with a pointed arch design—two on each side, a taller one at the back and a small square one by the front entry. He inserted clear plastic for the windows and put a wooden cross shape in the window behind the pulpit. He painted the outside and inside of the walls, added a chimney and a typical steeple, complete with a belfry. Once he had assembled the walls, he installed a yellow Christmas tree light and tested it before affixing the roof firmly in place. He could hardly wait to see Gerry's face when he brought it to him.

That was never to be. As Joe and Pat had faced their own devastation not long before, my world fell apart the following summer. One July day, Gerry was called to visit a nephew in trouble with the law, who was more desperate than anyone could have imagined. When Gerry went to talk with him, his nephew inexplicably shot and killed him, stole his car and took off. I waited for Gerry to come home for supper, and instead a Mountie arrived at my door to break the unbearable news that my husband was dead.

It was a month before the nephew was found and arrested. Alone with my two small sons, it was a dark time of grief and uncertainty, not knowing if my family was in danger, not comprehending why this had happened. I was thankful for friends and family who helped me through the fog of grief and trauma. To one trauma others were added: the death of my father-in-law, the trial of my husband's killer and then —both trauma and joy—the birth of my third child, a girl. Yet through all the chaos of those months, the Lord gave me an astounding sense of peace and His presence with me. I knew that my children and I were safe in His love.

When Joe heard the startling news of Gerry's death, he was devastated. He set the little church aside in a dark corner of his workroom. Nothing seemed to matter. Some months later, his daughter, Janet, said, "Dad, why don't you give the church to Gerry's widow? I'm sure it would mean something to her."

And so it was that Janet showed up at my door and told the story of how Joe had built this miniature church for Gerry. Lifting it out of the box, I held the lovely replica that was so similar to the country church my husband had pastored: his first and only church. We plugged it in and peeked inside. My two little boys and I "oohed" and "aahed" as we noticed different features.

Two-year old Ben peered through the clear windows at the side. "Where's people?"

"Look, Mommy!" cried my four-year-old, "You can open the teensy door."

"Oh, my goodness, there's even a pulpit and an organ," I exclaimed.

Gerry's visit and care for them was like a light in Joe and Pat's darkness. I never got to thank Joe in person for the gift of that church he so skillfully built and the joy it brought to me in my darkness. I have often peeked inside the church and watched my children and now my grandchildren do the same. There is a delight and a longing when we peer through those wee windows to a place we cannot enter. It's similar to the sweetness of remembering one who was precious, and the ache of longing to be together once more.

Miraculously, that original light bulb has never burnt out. The light within continues to illuminate the miniature church year after year, as inviting as the light that shone in Gerry's joyful, faith-filled life. I'm sure some day the light in the model church will burn out. But through faith in God, in our joys and in our longings over the years, there is a light within that will always shine in the darkness, and the darkness will never overcome it.

A CHRONICLE OF FARM, FAITH, AND CREATIVITY

H. M. RICHARDSON

Everyone's life has many challenges—little girls struggling with friendships, adolescents puzzling over what love is, grown women balancing work and parenting responsibilities. These experiences are common to people everywhere. Perhaps the biggest challenge in life, however, is learning how to follow the Lord with constancy in unanticipated circumstances.

From a very young age, I was a storyteller and an insatiable reader. I wasn't an only child by the strict definition, but my siblings weren't really playmates since they were five and eight years older than me. Fortunately, we sometimes had foster kids and neighbour kids to play with. It was difficult trying to get them to act out some of my imaginary plays!

I did very well in school as far as reading and writing were concerned. I should have kept some of those early stories because they got great marks and were often read aloud by the teacher. I won small writing trophies and a province-wide contest when my creative writing teacher asked permission to enter a sonnet I'd written. The contest called for poetry written in the style of Dylan Thomas. It was embarrassing to be called up in front of the school after my win and asked how long I had been reading Thomas's work. I had never read any of it!

After I left home, I tried to do some creative writing. I bought a typewriter, but typing and writing longhand took too long. I didn't have a computer until I was married with a family—one toddler and another baby on the way. Guess how much writing I did then? Not much.

As a city girl married to a country boy, I faced many predictable challenges. Among them were learning to decipher "farm–speak," coping with culture shock, and trying to run farm equipment. Take, for instance, the first time I ran a round baler. I had a great deal of trouble with the two levers that were right next to one another. One wrapped the bale in twine, and the other kicked the nicely bound and finished bale out of the machine. Unfortunately, I often got the two levers mixed up. I'll never forget the jaded expression of a hawk sitting on a nearby bale watching me kick out yet another unwrapped round of hay in front of its unbelieving eyes.

Fortunately, these first "Green Acres" hazards of inexperience diminished with time. But understanding the culture? I'm not there yet! I wish I'd realized at the start that this could have been my "mission field." At twenty–seven, I was only ten years a Christian and still too shy to approach strangers. (Writers are introverts, right?) I wish I could start over with what I know now after thirty–six years on the farm. But the road was long and convoluted.

As a young family, we followed the "wisdom" of those around us, which urged us to expand, expand, expand! We did okay for a time, farming along with my brother-in-law, except my husband had to work off the farm from 1987 to 2000 because there wasn't enough income for two families. Ron did many different jobs. Unfortunately, this took him out of the house, and our three girls never had the advantage of having Daddo around each day. (We were always called "Mommo" and "Daddo".)

I didn't do much writing until our girls were older. I finished a historical novella about knights in shining armour, but I couldn't find anyone interested in publishing it. The real story of my heart, the one that grew out of all my soul's struggles and was a catharsis to write, kept revolving in my mind. The very first concepts of it were seeded when I was about eighteen and evolved through many years and a lot of rough drafts.

I tried to supplement our farm income by working outside the home, but it isn't easy when you are far from a large city. My career before marriage was working at the Calgary head office of Wycliffe Bible Translators as a video producer, chronicling the lives of missionaries. There was nothing going on in that vein in Olds until much later. When our children started to come, I quit off-farm work. Ron and I felt our little ones needed me at home. We had three girls, born in 1990, '93, and '95. I often despaired, as young moms do, over the fact that I was doing nothing more than changing diapers, feeding faces, and cleaning up messes. Ron once asked me, when he got home, if I had mopped the floor with Kool-Aid. I said, "Yes, basically." It was a whole jug of spilled juice!

From 2000 to 2004, we began exporting hay through the Transfeeder's export company. We thought we had made it big selling hay to Japan, as they were paying very good prices for feed. We also had 140 cows at the time. We rented land and started haying on a grand scale with 700 acres and a paid haying crew. All might have worked out just fine, but it didn't. Farmers often need to roll with the punches—but not three in a row!

In 2002, our crop of hay diminished to seventy percent of the usual yield. In 2003, it dwindled to fifty percent. That summer was declared the worst drought in recorded history. We borrowed money and bought 180 more cows to help compensate for this loss of income. Punch number one.

Then the second punch came in 2003. One dead cow in Alberta was tested for BSE (Mad Cow Disease) and came up positive. The United States slammed their border shut overnight to all Canadian beef, and our cattle lost seventy-five percent of their usual value.

The third disaster? In 2004 to 2005, the bottom dropped out of the hay market and Transfeeder Exports went broke. Three strikes and we were out! By December of 2007, the bank wanted us to put up our land for collateral, like a second mortgage, but we said no—so they took away our operating loan. Goodbye cows and farewell machinery.

God was faithful, though. We kept our land and home through the generosity of a family member. But the losses were too heavy. What could a creative like me do in these circumstances? Not a lot! I panicked and got a job at the Olds Municipal Library for 17 hours a week. I'd attended a writer's group there once. It was a great place to work, but I barely made enough for groceries.

Have you ever felt that the Lord has led you out on a limb and then cut the branch off behind you? That was us. Ron went out to work again. For a long time, we felt abandoned by God. Neither of us seemed to be doing what we should. Eventually, we learned that when the Lord has "broken your heart," He is really calling you into a different life with a brand-new understanding that nothing can separate you from His love. In 2018, Ron began to pray and followed heavenly directions into a new home-based business.

For me, God turned COVID-19 into a blessing. During that crazy time, I found self-publishing training online because I was doing more trolling on the internet. God opened that door for me, asking me to dust off my writing files for one more look. I had nothing else to do! He revived the publishing dreams I thought were long dead. I needed some money to begin, and He provided that! And at last, that long-ago story concept that had begun in my youth began to take shape. At the end of December 2021, after a truckload of work, I finished my story revisions and published two books in a series for young adults called *Tower of the Deep*. (And I'm not done yet!)

Now grandparents, God has brought us to a place where we use sixties–era machines to put up small square bales for horse hay, for a nice profit. It keeps Ron fit and healthy. God led both of us toward new horizons! We now follow Him truly and trust Him to provide for us, day by day.

REFLECTIONS ON THE END OF LIFE

ALAN ANDERSON

> *"Therefore we do not lose heart. Though outwardly we are wasting away, yet inwardly we are being renewed day by day. For our light and momentary troubles are achieving for us an eternal glory that far outweighs them all. So we fix our eyes not on what is seen, but on what is unseen, since what is seen is temporary, but what is unseen is eternal" (*2 Corinthians 4:16-18*).*

In this memoir account, I share how my background as a local church pastor and healthcare chaplain helped shape me as a writer. My calling, especially as a healthcare chaplain, focused on end-of-life care. I worked in long-term care facilities, where the average age of people was eighty-four years. In the healthcare language, they were called "patients" or "residents." I called them my "Teachers."

As I have walked, run, and even crawled through life, these past few years have continued to teach me more about living. My Teachers have been the source of most of what I have learned and hopefully applied in life. Notice the capital letter, "T." This signifies my profound respect for these people, and the impact they have on me as I interact with the world today.

Winter Path by K. Payne

Lessons from My Teachers That Stay with Me

There is much a writer can learn about himself in the chaos that may accompany end-of-life situations. Here are a few lessons I now live by, which also help me develop my writing.

The Act of Listening

As a chaplain, interaction with my Teachers allowed me to sharpen my listening skills. Listening means more than hearing a person. When one listens to another person, one desires to understand the other through not only the sounds of words but also such things as one's tone of voice. If we do not listen to people, we will not know what, if anything, we are to say. If we do not listen, we do not show we care. Listening is crucial to one's interaction with people, especially those living with terminal illness. Profound yet simple insights about life come from those aware the end of their life is drawing near.

To listen as one writes is also crucial. As I write about experiences with my Teachers, I do so with a clear head and listening heart. I ask myself questions like, *What makes this experience of being with someone memorable?* I also try my best to choose the right words. As I sat by the bedsides of my Teachers, I always felt such an honour to be with them. When a poem or memoir account comes to mind, I write to honour those I sat with. I write words to capture the reality of the memory without drama or exaggeration.

Write with Empathy

My Teachers' stories pierced my heart. I would feel the spiritual or emotional pain they experienced as they told me their stories. I would thank them for their honesty and acknowledge their courage to share their stories with me. They stressed how their encounters with end-of-life suffering caused them to acknowledge what matters in life. These meetings made me ponder my life and assess if I'm focusing on the right things.

Empathy is a component of my writing. In my approach to what I write, I want to convey I have been present with people. My hope is this empathic way of writing will bring a sense of authenticity to readers. Times of chaos need not rule out a need for empathy. One's ability to empathize with people even at a time of a person's last hours will strengthen one's ability as a storyteller.

Write in an Honest and Real Manner

Write words that show you have been with people at the end of life. Not everyone faces their end-of-life news in a passive manner or with acceptance. While, in my experience, most people did, I can also say there were times when one of my Teachers went into utter emotional chaos. This is the point where a chaplain's mettle is tested. This is a challenge to find peace, calmness, and an honest response in the face of a person's soon demise.

When writing about lessons from my Teachers, I am honest. I do not make outcomes of end-of-life news sound like everything works out well. I do, however, allow my words to pour out honest emotions. The words I use reflect the emotions and chaos that often accompany end-of-life experiences.

Recognize One's Vulnerability

If someone chooses to work in an end-of-life setting, they must recognize their own vulnerability and the chaos of being human. When I worked as a chaplain, it didn't take long for me to come to grips with the fact I will one day die. Although this might sound obvious, how a writer responds to this reality will prove the sincerity of his writing.

When I write, the memories of my Teachers are the ink which flows from my pen. This motivates me to write with integrity. Perhaps one day a memory of me will be the ink of a writer's pen.

Haunted Words

Sometimes words of others stay with me and, in a sense, haunt me. I capture these words in my written work. My writing comprises poetry or prose inspired by real-life experiences. I remember, while taking chaplaincy clinical training at a local hospital, I read words in the hospital chapel from a mother. She wrote in the memory book on the stand close to the front of the chapel. Her words poured from a broken heart. She asked God to forgive her for not taking care of her son, who had died from a drug overdose that day.

The words of this mother haunted me for a long time. Although years have gone by, I still remember what she wrote: "God, forgive me for not taking care of the gift you gave me in my son." As a writer, I must not hide from words which may haunt but turn them into words of hope.

Focus on Prayer

Silence and stillness are companions in end-of-life care situations. A tone of silence and stillness also accompanies my writing. Prayer bathes the words I write relative to my calling. I pray the words are the right ones. I also pray my words encourage and comfort those who need or welcome them.

Where Broken Words Belong

Occasionally, I write broken words. The words, in need of love and a place where they belong, weep and collapse on the page. They stream from a writer aware of his own frailty. Ministry to people near the end of life teaches this reality by being in their presence. Most of my Teachers seemed to accept their brokenness and the reality of their terminal illness. Some struggled with the truth, but they accepted their end was near. The words I write belong in the world to help broken people heal. With this healing, there is hope in God to encourage people not to lose heart.

Reflections on My Teachers

Many of my Teachers were Christian people who did not hide their grief, pain, or suffering. I heard their cries and their laughter. I saw the sorrow etched on their faces as they looked back on life with their families. They also shared the sure hope they would soon be with God, and this made their countenances shine.

Writers who are Christians can show the world brokenness and chaos does not mean defeat. We can bring hope and healing to our readers through the words we write. This means we do not lose heart, we do not quit, and we do not waste our brokenness. My Teachers were also healers. They taught me that the beautiful reality of one's life matters, despite the chaos of the world. We can all be healers, for we are all Teachers.

Faith in God has kept me focused. Focused on a calling rich with memories of people who were not afraid to share with me their private thoughts about the end of their life. Lessons from my Teachers are one of the main reason I write what I write.

As the years have flown by and I look back on my Teachers, I cherish the legacies they have passed on to me. I live my life as best as I can, despite the uncertainty of its duration. This includes my calling as a writer. If my mind ever becomes unable to write, I hope I've passed on at least some of what my Teachers taught me.

Be A Healer

by Alan Anderson

Be a healer,
Turn coarse words into healing balm.
Look beyond narratives meant to cripple.
Show the way to peace, true peace,
beyond understanding,
Soaked in love.

Shoulders of healers,
Are where those with weary heads rest.
Outstretched arms provide an oasis for hugs,
Closeness allows hearts to beat together.

Walk into the world to live what love is,
Hold the hands of those who stumble,
Those who fall in the darkness,
For we are all broken.

WRITING BLIND

SCOTT FITZSIMMONS

I spent the last twenty years living in Yorkton, Saskatchewan. Fifteen of those were spent as the program Director for The ROCK98Five, a Christian radio station. I love radio! However, I love Christian music more.

The reason I am no longer employed at The ROCK is because of a bout with Acute Lymphoblastic Leukemia. It was a diagnosis that came out of nowhere in May 2019.

Since different types of cancer have touched the lives of so many people for so long, it's hard to be surprised by the treatment process. It's just chemo and radiation, right? I know I say that all nonchalant like, and I don't want to lessen the effect of it, but there are generally common side effects. For example, hair loss, nausea, pain, and malaise. There are different types of chemotherapy, and there are various doses of radiation. Sometimes there is surgery, and there are new treatments coming out very regularly.

I did go through everything except surgery, but there was one thing I didn't expect, and for that matter, neither did the doctors.

I was recovering from a stem cell transplant and starting to get healthy and strong again. I was walking lots. I was cooking, barbecuing, and starting to live life again! I had even started writing a book after a friend suggested I do so.

It was in September 2020 that I noticed my eyes were doing some funny things. I was having cloudy vision, which was somewhat concerning. By December that year, I was diagnosed as legally blind.

From going through treatments, incluing radiation therapy, in the first stage of my cancer to going through stem cell transplant, I could still watch TV, listen to music, and write whenever I got a chance. But now that my sight was almost gone, although I could still listen to music, TV shows, and movies, I didn't know how to keep going with my writing.

After being contacted by the CNIB, the Canadian National Institute for the Blind, I was given good ideas on how to move forward with the use of technology. I was quite confident in using computers and my smartphone before losing my sight, but the help they gave me was greatly appreciated. I left their office with a good starting point for understanding how to navigate new software. Some programs worked well, some took a while, but others I've given up on for now. This organization was a godsend in helping me focus my efforts instead of feeling frustrated when I couldn't operate my devices properly.

I soon figured out how I could use dictation to record my thoughts on a digital document. Being a stickler for format and proper sentence structure, this process was not easy for me. I finally realized that to get my thoughts out as best as I could, I needed to let go of editing on the fly. It was vital to get my thoughts onto the page and fix the dictation mistakes later. This turned out to be a very productive choice. Dictation did an adequate job of capturing what I was trying to get across. Then when help arrived, editing would be an easy or relatively easy task.

During my life, I have found talking through my struggles has been the best way for me to deal with my emotions. I never kept a journal, but I often wrote letters, articles, or social media posts to share how I felt. When the idea for my book came around, this became my "journal."

Once I got the words flowing out of my mouth and onto the page through dictation, many of my memories of the past five years came back with great clarity. Speaking those words almost became addictive. At first, I felt it might be hard to fill a chapter. However, those feelings were quashed early on because my gift of gab translated nicely to writing and giving as much detail as possible. It became something I greatly looked forward to daily. After setting a goal of one hour a day, it didn't take long for me to regularly surpass that goal.

Looking back on all the different stages of my cancer battle and subsequent health struggles allowed me to understand that, while difficult in the moment, they weren't as problematic in the long run. Plus, looking back at many of the positive experiences regularly brought a smile to my face.

Losing my sight was the hardest part of this whole process. Yet, what was most interesting was the discovery that losing my sight and having to focus to properly get my thoughts out actually helped me be more productive. It helped me become more streamlined in keeping my thoughts together in one place instead of in multiple documents or posts over different platforms.

Being visually impaired has its Jekyll and Hyde moments. On the one hand, I like trying to find out how I can do some of the things I did before and learn new things I hadn't thought of doing in the past. However, it doesn't take long to realize there are many things with which I need help from others. Patience doesn't come easily when all you used to do is stalled by the absence of someone to help you complete your project. The hardest part is when something you've been doing for a while, specifically on your smartphone, gets changed.

Now you must spend a long time figuring out what has changed, why it has changed, and how you can use it after the change. How ironic is it that the tool I used to help me in my darkest times can also be my greatest adversary?

God has given me a valuable outlet to process what I am going through in this stage of my life. Writing has offered more opportunities to get my frustrations out, share my small victories, and even have a laugh at some of my gaffes and bloopers. I often see myself through a different lens when I put my words on paper. I can see where what seemed to be a failure turned out to be a win! In the moment, it can be hard to see, but reading back the words on the page helps me find little flowers in the desert.

Spending time writing allows me the opportunity to keep thinking about what I am going to do next, which keeps my mind busy and away from negative thoughts or just plain idleness. It also keeps me from finding things to just pass the time. It can be very easy to sit back and have TV, social media, sports, politics, etc., fill your mind for hours on end. Then you feel like you have nothing to show for your day. Writing keeps me moving forward and encourages me. Writing also keeps my mind focused on what else I can learn as a writer. I know I can tell a story, especially from my own perspective, but how am I going to expand into genres I hadn't thought of trying in the past? Writing often takes the place of anxious thoughts and "what if" questions that pop up.

Most of all, writing has given me an opportunity to do something with my life that is much greater than I ever thought I could do as a blind person. God has not only used my blindness to help me get closer to Him, but also to share what He has done in my life with an even greater audience than I ever could have expected! I have always loved to preach, and I often still do. I have so many ideas in my mind. I've started writing them down and look forward to using them in future writing projects. It is funny, though, that while I have moved from speaking on the radio to writing on paper, I still need to use my voice to speak into my phone to share my thoughts. The medium has changed, but just because I'm no longer on the radio doesn't mean God can't use me and my voice.

PART SEVEN
POETRY

Woods by Connie Inglis

We Are God's Hands

By Maureen E Kowal

It is a meeting
And I come
Foot weary
Heart sore
I sit at a table
Alone
Then I heard the tread of feet
And shared laughter
A touch upon my shoulder
A smile warm and tender
I reach out and feel the softness of the quilt
The point of the needle
And we are off
Stitching amid jokes and bits of hymns
Until it is done and sent away
And now . . .
In a hospital
Ripped open paper reveals
A quilt taken with trembling hands
Gazing at flowing colours
And wrapped around cold shoulders
We are God's hands

♥∴~∴♥∴~∴♥

ECHO

By Janey Bordihn

There is a resonance deep within
that sings to me in a beautiful pitch,
echoing a faint melody of something I once knew.

It haunts me with a memory I have long forgotten
or possibly one waiting yet to be—
I don't know which.

It plays beneath the hum and rhythm
and cadence of my life,
Lower still
than the tyrannical din of responsibilities and shoulds.
But yet, I feel its presence.
I know its voice.

A song, a call, a reproach, a reminder,
whispering to my mind an urgent longing—

Take this moment, with its thoughts, chaos and beauty
. . . and write it down.

A Hum

By Lorraine Boerchers

A hum, a vibration.
What is this feeling?
Agitation, restlessness.
Is there something wrong?
I've been ignoring a need,
A need to create.
As the creativity flows,
The restlessness quiets,
A soothing hum remains.

Stillness

By Carol Harrison

Unbroken by screeching sirens
or vehicles whizzing past,
near silence falls.
Even the cocky blue jay
hides deep
in the old evergreen.
No raucous caws
from crows perched
on the light posts.
Chaos forgotten
A ticking clock intrudes,
marking time's passage
as I wait in the quietness
for inspiration.

♥~~~♥~~~♥

A Novel Apprehension
By Irene Worster-LoScerbo

Mark my words, reader!
They break and enter closed minds,
stealing hearts and all.

Catch phrases in acts of verbal abuse.
Quiet the chaos.
Sentence it to life!

Watch punctuation
untangle verbosity.
Make it tow the story line.

Bound in secrecy,
truth is stranger than fiction.
Conviction acquits.

Yes, the words are out,
out on parole,
to wake, to warn, to woo you.

Read between the lines.
They've turned over a new leaf.
Open and shut case.

♥∻♥∻♥

Cloudburst

By L. Marie Enns

In times of adversity, I tend to keep mulling over the problem that dominates my thoughts and steals my peace and joy. Finally, I find relief by putting my thoughts into words. The problem may still not be solved, but once I have expressed my feelings, I can go on with life while I wait for a solution.

Oh, Lord, when will the sun shine warm again,
dispelling all this murky gloom and rain?
A week ago, I basked in peaceful calm
until that angry storm cloud came along
and burst upon me with no warning. None!
Then left me reeling at what had been done.

So now my heart is heavy like that cloud,
my thoughts a jumble, voices prating loud,
my feelings wounded, in despairing pain,
emotions as unstable as the rain.
My mind is full of questions, and intense
to think of answers that will make some sense.

Oh, Lord, I try to pray and seek Your aid
but don't know what requests should now be made.
It seems there's no solution I can see
that would be satisfactory to me.
I pray You'll do whatever is Your will
and help me trust Your grace and goodness, still.

May I await the outcome patiently.
Let bitterness not find a home in me.
Help me forgive what others have done wrong
and once again to sing a praiseful song.
Then lead me from this dark and dreary place
to feel the warming sunshine of Your face!

♥∼∼∼♥∼∼∼♥

Come and See

By MaryAnn Ward

Crayons, stickers, and clay,
sandcastles, blocks, and blanket forts,
scissors, finger paints, and glue,
the makings of childhood efforts.
"Come and see."

Scrapbooks, collages, and tie-dye,
music, drama, and dance,
journals, secret diaries, and poems,
hammers, saws, and electric drills.
"Come and see."

Tapestry, weaving, and stitch,
oils, acrylics, and pastels,
mosaics, crown mouldings, and trim,
gardens, garages, and dens.
"Come and see."

Potters, masons, and architects,
artists and writers with skill,
carpenters, scientists, and dreamers,
designers, inspiring wonder and awe.
"Come and see."

What spurs such creative endeavours?
What drives perfection and style?
From where comes the urge to fashion —
making old into new, nothing into something?
"Come and see."

"Come and see,
The Creator of all."

♥∴~∴♥∴~∴♥

Roots

By Whitney Braun

Here I am again,
in the trenches.
Wet, stagnant trenches,
a war zone of trials.

Nothing grows here, roots drown
as the light is blocked by struggle.

Is this the life You planned for me?
Disregard of my fears,
ignorant about my aspirations,
intolerant of my queries.

A season that I can't explain,
life to the full far from my grasp.

Days and months of darkness
finally broken by a flicker,
as musty air gives way
to a gust of fresh hope.

My lungs fill with assurances
I'd given up on.
My veins open wide for Your Word
to spread and root deep.

From those roots spring new life,
full of colour, growth, and guarantees.
The deep breath I've been longing for,
the flourish I was promised.

The bloom of a new season
that started in the trenches.

Orphan

By Colleen Jantzen

I'm longing for connection
Are you
To feel like I belong
(really)

To

A place
A space
A people

This fractured world has fractured me and I

Repeat stories
Repeat stories
(not my own)

Trying to feel
At home

To tie a tie
(however tenuous)
To someone

Anyone

Who'll own me

A Humble Praise

By MaryAnn Ward

For such a wicked wretch as I,
For weak and frail You did die.
Upon Thy brow a thorny crown
As nail-scarred hands reached down.

How oft' I cease from humble praise
To thank You, Lord, with heart upraised.
Why should my tongue rest quiet still,
When rocks cry out from distant hill.

Praise Him you deaf, you dumb and weak.
Arise, arise to mountain's peak.
Fling wide the gates of praise and song,
For angels hushed stand viewing down.

For men to lift unceasing praise,
One by one their voices raise.
'til above the waves and thunder roll,
The glorious praise of God unfolds.

Then angels shout and
Hosannas ring.
Heaven and earth
Together sing.
Glory,
Glory,
Glory,
To the Lamb, our Lord and King.

Breadwinner

By Irene Worster-LoScerbo

one whose cupboard is bare
her last supper eaten
who in her despair
is sure she's been beaten

but you come along
with a loaf and a smile
and like slow dough that's rising
you linger awhile
put her life in perspective
pack into each slice
sweet jams, joys and jellies
hints of fresh herbs and spice

she has chewed, been renewed
having savoured each crumb
now her cup runneth over
she's no longer glum

♥~~~♥~~~♥

To Create

By Lorraine Boerchers

To take random words
and create a readable thought.
To put paint to canvas
and create a vista.
To take a piece of cotton
and create a garment.
To move a chair
and create a room.
To channel scattered ideas
down to one,
to process the idea
and make it real.
The inescapable need
the universal need
to create.

Drought's End

By Gail Neumann

Dust clouds rise around my feet
as I walk along the forest trail
even though the summer rain has spent all day
gently washing the faces of the rocks on the shore.

Fir and cedar branches bow low over my head
filled to overflowing with the water of life
but I am thirsty and dry.

I walk softly through the forest
listening to the steady dripping,
smelling the musky freshness.

An eagle cries from his perch
on a snag towering above the forest canopy.

I consider his song and abruptly I stop.
Praise for my Creator erupts within me
and grows until I begin to dance and sing.

The trees over my head let go of the rain
and showers of blessing pour over me.
I am soaked, dripping and laughing
and the dry land around me is satisfied.

A Desert Apatheia

By Nina Faye Morey

I came to dwell in the desert
drawn by the Spirit's call
to this womb of the Word
to live in peaceful solitude
hearing the voice of The Living God
in calm pregnant silence
yearning in my heart
for that fiery passionate union
confessed to by those other solitaries
living in their lonely desert cells

I came to listen in the desert
to that still small voice
of an immanent spirit
abiding deep within my flesh's core
stifling tirades from a troubling tyrant
who burdened me
with dead wood
and worried me
with such wild petrified timbre
of inner chaos and turmoil

I came to seek in the desert
an abundant simplicity of being
with suppression of this built-in barrenness
at the nucleus of my soul's vessel
discerning lessons from The Lord Who Sanctifies
in humble cloistered silence
feeling those consuming flames of purification
melting away my fleshly layers
in this blazing earthen crucible
becoming one with my Creator God

PART EIGHT
HOBBIES & HOME

Dragonfly by K. Payne

SHIRLEY'S ENERGY BITES

SANDI SOMERS

Out of nowhere, it seemed, I felt a deep burden to pray for Shirley.[1] I knew something was wrong, but I didn't know what. The Lord had placed that burden on me for a reason. For several days, I prayed and then arranged a time to visit her. Meanwhile, in reading the Psalms during my quiet time, I was drawn to pray these verses for Shirley: "Teach me how to live, O LORD. Lead me along the right path . . . Wait patiently for the LORD. Be brave and courageous (Psalm 27:11,14d NLT).

I almost jumped at the words, "Teach me how to live, O LORD." For these were almost the same words Joni Eareckson Tada prayed years ago during her darkest time after her paralyzing accident. Becoming a quadriplegic after a failed dive into a shallow pool, she prayed to be healed, but that was not to be. She became bitter and, in her lowest moments, wanted to die.

Joni lay in her dark room for two weeks until she realized she could not live with bitterness. "Oh Lord Jesus," she cried out, "if I can't die, then please show me how to live." She admitted that it was her first "honest to goodness prayer, not for healing necessarily, but for help from God."[2]

The morning I visited with Shirley, she shared with me the life she had built with her husband. After he passed, she was busy with legal issues, disposing of his personal effects, and learning to manage the farm on her own. Now, two years later, she felt no energy and she slept more than usual. Her spirit was heavy, and she struggled to find a meaningful purpose without her husband. This was not her usual self—energetic, buoyant, busy visiting neighbours and gifting them with her encouragement and fresh-baked buns. "What's wrong?" she asked. Obviously, she was deep in grief, and that had descended into depression.

As we chatted, she placed teacups and a plate of goodies—energy bites, she called them—on the table. I told her Joni Eareckson Tada's story and the verses the Lord had given me for her, particularly, "Teach me how to live, O LORD." Then, wrapping my arms around Shirley, I prayed for her—for the Lord to remove the depression and grief and to lift her spirits. He did just that.

And now, as I make energy bites, I pray for Shirley to find a new purpose and feel God's continuing presence in her life.

Shirley's Energy Bites

- 1 cup quick oatmeal
- 1/2 cup peanut butter
- 1/2 cup flax seeds (can exchange for any favourite nuts or seeds)
- 1/2 cup chocolate chips
- 1/3 cup honey
- 1 tsp. chia seeds (optional)
- 1 tsp. vanilla

Mix in a bowl.

Put a bit of oil or margarine on your hands and roll the mixture into small balls.

Keep them in the refrigerator so they remain cool and solid.

Enjoy!

Playing is happiness.
Have fun!

BRICK THERAPY

MARNIE POHLMANN

Lego Train by Marnie Pohlmann

For the longest time, I could not understand how someone going through a great struggle would not, or could not, read a book that promises help or comfort in their situation. I have lived in places where there were no counsellors, so assistance during troubled times was available only from God, friends, and books. I am an avid reader and writer, so I understand how words can touch our lives. Reading has always helped me to slow down, focus on problem solving and, more importantly, hear God's voice.

But then it happened to me!

A tsunami of troubles roaring down various valleys created a perfect superstorm in my life. I needed major surgery, my husband almost died, and we then found out he had an incurable cancer. The stressful job I loved was becoming overwhelming. My coping skills were failing, and my mental health deteriorated to deep depression. I might have managed these storms individually, but all at once, they exploded like lightning bolts—penetrating every vulnerable part of me.

With each deafening thunderclap resounding over top another, my heartbeat soon matched the pounding in my ears. I found no rest in the written word as I sought to find shelter. I read and reread the same paragraphs over and over. Oversized hailstones of confusion pummelled my mind. Nothing made sense. No words of encouragement or peace could pierce the foggy mist in my mind.

Not even my beloved books, including the Bible, which had always helped me in the past, came to my rescue. Neither music nor song offered any escape from the waves of pain and terror I was experiencing. Blank pages in my journal tormented me. My words were captive in the turmoil of my mind.

Then I discovered a new way to calm my heart and hear God speak.

I found I could let go of all my troubles when I played with building bricks! As a favourite toy for generations of children and adults alike, their longevity reassured me I will be okay. When the storms end, the damage can be rebuilt. A mess of bricks became creative joy from God's hand.

Yes, I am a grown woman. Yes, I have these sturdy bricks for my grandchildren to play with, but I also have sets that are just for me—from retro vehicles and buildings to a Christmas train. I enjoy the orchids and succulent plants that never need water; a red pickup truck with accessories to suit each season; and a small Dicken's *Christmas Carol* scene that sits on a bookshelf alongside the classic story. Displaying the sets is entertaining, but building them is what calms my storms.

When I am struggling, the tactile experience of sorting through the mixed sizes and shapes of these colourful bricks awakens my mind; it keeps me from racing into "what ifs." Their sharp and smooth edges help me name my pains and joys. I see possibilities with new creative combinations. The clatter of jumbled bricks reminds me chaos is simply part of the building process. Whether I am focusing on the instructions or figuring out how to build my own creation, my thoughts and heart settle. Order begins to rise from my inner chaos. The storm calms for a time, and I begin to hear God's voice as I snap brick pieces into place.

When I play with building bricks, I am learning to stand on a solid foundation throughout the storms of life. I find paths that lead me in new directions. My brokenness slowly builds to wholeness, and God-inspired repairs redeem the pain. Brick therapy is not only fun; it is one of the most helpful and creative ways I have experienced to quiet my mind and soul in times of trouble.

CHAOS IN THE GARDEN

SANDI SOMERS

Peonies from Canva Pro

It began with a dream. When I moved to my new house, I longed for a front yard brimming with curb appeal. I envisioned eye-catching flower beds bursting with beautiful plants and shrubs. I imagined designs that created elements of surprise around the next corner. And, more than anything, I wanted a yard that others could enjoy with me. I began, year by year, to develop my dreams.

But now, several years later, I walked through my yard and made plans for larger flower beds. Red begonias would complement my Hosta plants. I could see a pink hydrangea, a miniature rosebush, and peonies in the front corner by my entrance. Elsewhere, purple irises and large alliums would add colour to geraniums and coral bells. A showy silver-leafed dogwood shrub would fill an empty corner shaded by my next-door neighbour's tree. Shade-loving plants would fill in larger rings around my trees. I would even find a spot for evening scented stocks—plants that always graced my mom's yard.

Although my front yard showcases daffodils and tulips in the spring and geraniums throughout the summer, I wanted both my front and back yards to put on a spectacular show from early spring to late autumn. But as I looked over my yard, I grew disturbed by what I saw. Shrubs and trees had become overgrown and needed pruning. Flower beds were skimpy even in mid-summer. Perennials needed dividing or replacing. And the lawn required serious work to make it healthy and lush.

How had I let it get so overgrown and lacking in creativity? Why hadn't I done more over the years? I was an experienced gardener and had creative potential to make my yard a showpiece. When I first moved into this home, the previous owners had done little to develop the aesthetics. I loved to work in the soil; it gave me relaxation and a renewed touch with nature. But then constraints slowed my progress. I was still teaching. I travelled, and one summer I spent my non-working days being Mom's companion as her health failed. There were several summers when my own health issues prevented me from devoting energy and time to my flowers and garden.

And then there were the rabbits. I live in a newer area of Calgary, and houses began replacing the acreages around me. Coyotes, which had kept the rabbit population in check, moved farther away, and the rabbits began encroaching on our yards. One aggressive rabbit even hopped up on my porch and nibbled at my potted plants. In response, I became a minimalist and reduced my yard to plants my floral charts said were rabbit proof. What I had envisioned became a dashed dream; my dreams were being eaten!

I felt God prompting me to, once again, make my yard more attractive. What I envisioned would take all summer and beyond. Several nights, especially when overtired, I lay awake, the chaos in my spirit greater than the chaos in my yard. The restorative and developmental processes seemed epic. Was I trying to accomplish too much in one year? Would it be better to spread out my ambitions over several years rather than one season? In the beginning, I wanted to do everything on my own. I had to be honest. I am not a strong person physically, and my energies are not what they used to be now that I am a senior. It was one thing to have a vision and determination to see it through, but it was another to recognize my limitations.

I took my raw emotions to the Lord, yielding myself and my garden to Him. I recognized my being overwhelmed increased when I looked too far into the future rather than focusing on manageable daily tasks. I remembered what Thomas Carlyle, a British historian, said. "Our main business is not to see what lies dimly at a distance, but to do what lies clearly at hand."[1] And I remembered how our *InScribe Writers Online* bloggers once emphasized the necessity of taking small steps that would gradually accumulate into a satisfying creation.

I sensed the Lord telling me to start tackling what seemed impossible. During my devotional times, He gave me encouragement. "He fulfills the desires of those who fear him" (Psalm 145:19). He called me to go ahead. "Be strong and courageous and do the work. Do not be afraid or discouraged, for the LORD God, my God, is with you" (1 Chronicles 28:20). And He reminded me to "always pray and not give up" (Luke 18:1).

I realized then that God had given me this vision in the first place. I needed to develop my perseverance and keep my focus on the day-today venture while holding the future vision loosely. I yielded all my ideas, physical needs, and time to the Lord and began praying more specifically. "Come, Holy Spirit of wisdom and beauty. Please show me what to do." I asked Him to give me artistic designs and colourful, professional-looking flowerbeds that enhanced my yard from early spring through to late fall.

I brought out my gardening books and began mapping out flowers (mostly rabbit-proof!!) for each flower bed. On morning walks, I studied front yards and chatted with owners—some invited me into their back yards for a closer view. When my knees rebelled at the pressure of digging, I slowed my pace and admitted I could not do everything on my own. I reached out to others who enriched the entire process. I hired a teenager, Akashdeep, from across the street to xeriscape the patchy lawn edge. He had helped his father and grandfather to xeriscape their front yard, and I knew he had experience, strength, and willpower. When we finished the project in late October, Akashdeep was so proud. "I didn't know I could do all this," he said. This young man had done such an excellent job that I promised to give him a good reference when he began searching for employment.

On autumn days when I was not working in my yard, I visited garden centres to buy perennials and shrubs so they could get a head start the next spring. Neighbours stepped in to share their ideas, visualizing, planning, and mapping out areas to develop. Designing and positioning plants gave me a sense of moving forward and helped me visualize the end results.

Then God surprised me by extending the gardening season. While I know that the ground in Calgary usually freezes by late October, the weather was unusually warm until Christmas that year. What a delight to grab my edger and fork to enlarge flower beds—tasks that would facilitate projects the next spring.

I look back on that summer and fall as a time of learning. I needed to honour God with my ideas, creativity, and hard work. I needed to let go and trust Him during moments and days of unclarity. And I needed to work within my limits and allow others to be part of that creativity.

"The one who calls you is faithful, and he will do it" (1 Thessalonians 5:24).

PANDEMIC PIVOTING

SALLY MEADOWS

At the height of the pandemic, my husband and I sold our Saskatoon home of 27 years and moved across the country to New Brunswick. We anticipated there would be challenges, but little did we know how thoroughly our lives would be turned upside down. Starting over in a brand-new community 4000 km away is not for the faint of heart!

While my husband immersed himself in his new job, I looked forward to sharing my published books and my music with a whole new part of the country. But as COVID-19 restrictions continued and even tightened, opportunities to further my career as a writer, speaker, and musician were non-existent. To contribute to much-needed household income, I did the only thing that seemed feasible—I pivoted.

Upon my arrival in New Brunswick, I had a burning desire to create with my hands. After spending some time online doing research and taking a few courses, I experimented with a few fine crafts new to me. From upcycling dollar store items, to creating shell art "flower bouquets," to designing pressed flower art scenes, I leveraged resources that were readily available to create east-coast and nature-themed home décor that eventually sold in regional art galleries and tourist shops.

While my focus was visual art, I did not abandon my writing and music completely. I continued to write prose and songs, although less productively than during the years leading up to the pandemic. The highlight for me was recording two brand new songs with a top Canadian record producer who had moved back to his home province of New Brunswick when the pandemic struck. It was an amazing opportunity to work with someone I would never have otherwise if I had not moved to the East Coast.

There is no question that my time in New Brunswick was creatively productive—just not in the way I'd expected or hoped. While journalists contend that artists should not pivot during the pandemic, I believe I made the right choice for me. Pivoting allowed me the opportunity to try a few creative endeavours that were new and fresh to me while navigating our new normal in the midst of world chaos.

The COVID-19 pandemic is now behind us, but the memories of that time and what I learned remain. Regardless of external circumstances, it is always a good thing to learn a new craft, art, or skill. So, for those who are interested and willing to try something new in their own trying times, here are instructions on how to decoupage, make pressed flower art, and make shell art.

HOW TO DECOUPAGE

Supplies:

1. Any flat or gently curved surface that is smooth, such as glass, wood, canvas, plastic, metal, chipboard, heavy cardstock, ceramic, flat rocks, and the interior of flat seashells
2. A paper napkin, preferably with a white background, with an image you like that fits on your surface

3. Scissors
4. Fine paintbrush and water
5. White chalk paint
6. Paintbrush (for applying chalk paint)
7. Mod Podge
8. Flat nylon/decoupage brush
9. Plastic wrap
10. Ultra matte varnish
11. Flat paintbrush to apply varnish

A jar from a dollar or thrift store plus a pretty napkin is a trendy way to create lovely decoupaged home decor. Original photo by Sally Meadows.

Process:

1. Cut a piece of plastic wrap slightly larger than your napkin image to use in step 7.
2. Paint one or two coats of chalk paint on your surface, as much as needed for full opaque coverage (skip this step if your surface is white). Let dry.
3. Using the fine paintbrush and water, "paint" around your napkin image(s) about 1 cm away from the image's edges then tear your image(s) along the water line.

4. Gently pull off the upper layer of your napkin. (Most napkins have 2-3 layers.)
5. Using the flat decoupage brush and Mod Podge, generously coat the area on the surface where you want to place your image. Use your paintbrush to smooth out the Mod Podge to an area slightly bigger than your image.
6. Immediately place your napkin image on the surface, holding it as taut as possible to avoid wrinkles, and gently press it down in the centre with one or two fingers.
7. Place the plastic wrap over the image and start smoothing out the napkin onto the surface, moving your fingers from the centre of the image to the edges.
8. Wait a few minutes for partial drying, then add a thin coat of Mod Podge overtop with gentle strokes from the centre of the image outwards. Let dry. Add another coat; let dry.
9. Paint two thin layers of varnish over top, letting dry in between coats.

Pressed flower art (meadow scene) in a "float" frame. Original art and photo by Sally Meadows.

HOW TO MAKE PRESSED FLOWER ART

Supplies

1. Picture frame with two sheets of glass (no backing; often called "float frames")
2. Pressed flowers and/or leaves (can be purchased from Amazon; to press your own, see YouTube for how-to ideas)
3. Toothpick and white glue OR double-sided tape
4. White paper cut to the size of the glass
5. Tweezers
6. Window cleaner

Process:

1. Clean the glass plates in the frame thoroughly using the window cleaner.
2. Use the tweezers to pick up each pressed flower or leaf to assemble a design, picture, or montage on the white paper. Adjust as needed.
3. Element by element, transfer your design to one of the glass plates, adhering each element to the glass using tiny pieces of double-sided tape or white glue and a toothpick. It is not necessary to put glue or tape on the entire element, just the centre is sufficient. Let dry.
4. Gently place the second glass plate on top, sandwiching the elements inside and sliding both plates carefully back into the frame.

Floral bouquet with "flowers" created using seashells in a shadowbox. Original art and photo by Sally Meadows.

HOW TO CREATE SHELL ART

Supplies:

1. A variety of shells
2. A shadowbox
3. Glue that is strong enough to hold the shells in place
4. Card stock cut to the size of the shadowbox for the backing

Process:

1. Remove the back of the shadowbox.
2. Adhere the card stock to it.
3. Arrange your shells on the card stock in a geometric pattern or create a scene.
4. Glue the elements one by one. Let dry, confirming that each element is secure.
5. Insert the back into the shadowbox.

NOTES

LESS THAN A CARPENTER

1. Jules Supervielle, "La mer secrète," in *La Fable du Monde, poèmes* (Paris: Librairie Gallimard, 1938), 150.
2. Isak Dinesen (Karen Blixen), "Deluge at Norderney," in *Seven Gothic Tales*, Kindle Edition (Avarang Books, 2023), location 709.
3. Sarah Williams ("Sadie"), "Is it so, O Christ in heaven," in Towner's Male Choir Combined (Chicago/New York/Toronto: Fleming H. Revell Company, 1894), 85.

TRANSFORMING DARKNESS INTO LIGHT

1. Franz Kafka, Letter to Oskar Pollak (27 Jan 1904)

MIDNIGHT PRAISES

1. Name changed for privacy.
2. https://www.healthline.com/health/benefits-of-singing#benefits accessed January 11, 2024.

THE ART OF FACING CHAOS

1. Stanley Fish, *How to Write a Sentence: and How to Read One* (New York: Harper Collins, 2011), p.4.
2. Anthony Burgess, *Enderby Outside* (London: William Heinemann, 1968).

FINDING HOPE

1. Henry Wadsworth Longfellow, "Proem," in *The Waif: A Collection of Poems,* 5th edition. (Boston: William D. Ticknor & Co., 1846), xi

DEVELOPING A CREATIVE LIFESTYLE IN TRYING TIMES

1. Wikipedia.org https://en.wikipedia.org/wiki/Writing_therapy
2. Bessel van der Kolk, *The Body Keeps the Score: Brain, Mind, and Body in the Healing of Trauma,* (New York: Penguin Books, 2014).

3. Scott Barry Kaufman, https://blogs.scientificamerican.com/beautiful-minds/the-creative-life-and-well-being/

SHIRLEY'S ENERGY BITES

1. Name changed for privacy.
2. Joni Eareckson Tada, "Owning Your Weakness", Centre Street Church, Calgary, Alberta, June 5, 2016, https://www.cschurch.ca/sermons/?speaker=joni-erickson tada

CHAOS IN THE GARDEN

1. https://dailywriterlife.com/do-whats-in-front-of-you-2/ Accessed August 26, 2023.

History of ICWF: Celebrating Our 25th Anniversary of InScribe

NINA FAYE MOREY

InScribe Christian Writers' Fellowship (ICWF) has been "encouraging Canadian Christian writers for over 25 years." Our roots go back to the creation of the Central Alberta Christian Writers group by 12 Alberta writers attending the Decision School of Christian Writing in Calgary in July 1979. June Bevan, then from Rocky Mountain House, urged this group of fellow writers to start a provincial writers' group, "We need to do something like this in Alberta." Along with June, Sophie Thunell and Ruth Vikse became the founding board members, forming an executive committee with June Bevan serving as the first president.

The purpose of this fledgling writers' group was "to provide a vehicle for mutual support, stimulation, and growth for Christian writers in Alberta." Their primary objective was to sponsor an annual conference for Alberta Christian writers. Their first conference, held on November 8, 1980, was at the Canadian Lutheran Bible Institute in Camrose. Sixty-six writers attended, far exceeding their expectations.

They held their second conference at the same venue in 1981. There were 42 writers in attendance from all over the province, 22 of them paid-up members. (The membership fee was $15.) At this conference, they officially changed their name to the Alberta Christian Writers' Fellowship (ACWF). The word "Fellowship" reflected their core values of mentorship, relationship, and community. June Bevan continued as President, followed over the years by Sophie Thunell, Alice Cundiff, Sophie Stark, Lavyne Osbak, Dr. Gerald Hankins, and Elsie Montgomery.

Subsequent fall conferences in the 1980s were held at Camp Kuriakos on Sylvan Lake, Lacombe Nazarene Church, Oriole Park Missionary Church in Red Deer, North American Baptist College (NABC) in Edmonton, and the Grey Nuns Regional Centre in Edmonton. ACWF's 10th anniversary was celebrated at the Hospitality Inn in Calgary in October 1989.

These initial conferences, like today's, featured a variety of workshop topics, including poetry, fiction, nonfiction, and devotionals. Rudy Wiebe and John Patrick Gillese were two early keynote speakers. In 1987, Maxine Hancock delivered the opening address at the NABC in Edmonton. There were 125 in attendance. Membership increased from 32 that year to 98 in 1988.

ACWF's first satellite writing group was formed at Barbara Mitchell's Calgary home on September 15, 1986. Its successor, ICWF, currently has fifteen local writing groups across Canada overseen by a Writing Groups Coordinator. In April 1990, the first Spring Workshop was held at Oriole Park Church in Red Deer. In 1996, Marcia Lee Laycock suggested these annual workshops be renamed Spring WorDshops, and they continue to be a fun way for members to get together with other local writers to hone their writing skills.

In the early 1990s, fall conferences were held once more at the Grey Nuns Regional Center, twice at the Prairie Bible Institute (Three Hills), and at the Star of the North Retreat Centre in St. Albert in 1993 with Janette Oke speaking on Friday evening and Marge and Bernard Palmer on Saturday. It was back to Camp Kuriakos in 1994 with Maxine Hancock and Phil Callaway as guest speakers. Lorna Dueck was the plenary speaker in 1995 at King's University College in Edmonton. There have been many insightful, inspiring, and engaging keynote speakers over the years. Les Stobbe in 1999, Janette Oke again in 2000, Phil Callaway in 2001 and 2014, Linda Hall in 2001 and 2016, Murray Pura in 2005 and 2013, Sigmund Brouwer in 2010 and 2019, Grace Fox in 2011 and 2022, and Steve Bell and Ellen Duffield in 2023, to name just a few.

In the fall of 1996, ACWF expanded across Canada, changing its name to ACWF-Canada Wide. Elsie Montgomery continued serving as President from 1998-99. In 1999, the name changed again to InScribe Christian Writers' Fellowship (ICWF). In January 2020, ICWF was incorporated as a non-profit society under the Society's Act of the Government of Alberta. Members who have served as ICWF President over the years include Marcia Lee Laycock, Eunice Matchett, Lisa Wojna, Jack Popjes, Ruth L. Snyder, Tracy Krauss, Sheila Webster, and Barbara Fuller.

In 1999, InScribe registered its domain name *InScribe.org* and created a website. To facilitate communication between members, an online discussion group and later a Yahoo Listserv email group were introduced. In November 2006, we launched our first public InScribe blog where members post on faith and writing and receive feedback at https://inscribewritersonline.blogspot.com/ A second InScribe Professional Blog, https://inscribe.org/category/blog/, to share information and advice on writing was added to our website in 2014. Although InScribe members from across Canada may never meet in person, these online resources help them connect with and support fellow Christian writers.

To celebrate the Fellowship's 20th anniversary in 2000, Nathan Harms published the book, *Companion*, featuring stories and photos of our history. Members were encouraged to contribute a biographical page. Four Alberta writers, Phil Callaway, Linda Hall, Maxine Hancock, and Janette Oke, were the featured speakers, addressing the theme "Celebrate the Word," at the InScribe Fall Conference that year.

ACWF annual conferences were initially held on Saturdays. Eventually, Friday evening sessions were added. ICWF Fall Conferences have now grown to include a Thursday evening authors' social event with readings. Friday and Saturday events include keynote speakers and workshop sessions, along with a Friday evening awards banquet. In earlier years, Wisemen's Way Bookstore in Camrose hosted a book display and sale. InScribe's Fall Conferences now include book tables where members can display and sell their books. ACWF's first conference writing contests were introduced in 1983 and judged by Alberta Culture. These Fall Writing Contests continue to be a popular feature of InScribe conferences. Winners of selected genres are chosen by experienced judges and presented certificates and cash prizes at the awards banquet.

Over the years, InScribe has increased the number of awards and bursaries available. Members can now apply or be nominated for the Barnabas Award, the Janette Oke Award, the Editor's Choice Award, and the Leadership Award. The Barnabas Award, founded by Dr. Gerald Hankins, awards a grant of $250 annually to encourage and assist writers in their writing careers. The Janette Oke Award, introduced in 2016 to honour founding and lifetime member, Janette Oke, is presented bi-annually to a member who demonstrates a strong Christian commitment and innovation in their chosen genre. This award is a minimum of $250, depending on donations. The Leadership Award of $100 is presented to a nominee who has demonstrated leadership qualities and contributed to InScribe over an extended period. The Editor's Choice Award, founded by Nina Faye Morey, is a $100 annual award for an outstanding piece published in *FellowScript* since the previous fall conference.

InScribe's *FellowScript* magazine began as the *ACWF Newsletter*, produced by Helena Brown in 1983. The retired Grade 1 teacher from Didsbury filled it with homey comments, encouraging words, scripture quotations, and information about conferences and contests. It has gradually grown from a single page sent to fifteen members to its current 32-page, print and e-magazine formats sent quarterly to over 100 members. A contest was held in 1993 to determine the new magazine's name and the winning entry, *FellowScript*, was submitted by Marion Jackson. The magazine provides an opportunity for members to publish (and receive payment for) their writing. For several years, a separate *FellowScript Fall Supplement* was published to report on the events and awards presented at InScribe's Fall conference and display the writing of the Fall Contest winners. These are now incorporated into the November issue of *FellowScript*. InScribe also produces a monthly email newsletter, *InSide InScribe*, to share news and information with its members.

In addition to *FellowScipt* magazine, InScribe has published four previous anthologies showcasing our members' writing. The first, *InScribed: 30 Years of Inspiring Writers*, was published by Forever Books in 2010. In the introduction, long-time member, Marcia Lee Laycock, expresses a sentiment held by most InScribe members: "I owe them a debt I could never repay, for their friendship, their commitment to the call to write and dedication to training and empowering writers of faith." In 2015, InScribe Press published their second anthology, *7 Essential Habits of Christian Writers*, addressing seven key areas deemed essential for Christian writers to succeed. InScribe Press's third anthology, *Christmas: Stories & More*, was published in 2017 to encourage readers to reflect on the beauty and blessings of this season. Following up on its success, InScribe Press published *Easter: Stories & More* in 2021, featuring the work of forty talented members from across Canada. It encourages readers to reflect on this holy season's themes of forgiveness, salvation, grace, and hope.

God's blessing has been evident throughout ICWF's history, and our Fellowship has become a widely recognized force in Christian writing and publishing. We sincerely thank the dedicated executive, associate executive, and other volunteer members who have faithfully served us over these many years. We look back on our history with gratitude, and we continue to seek God's guidance as we stimulate, encourage, and support Christians who write.

—Derived from previous histories written by Shirley Kolanchey, Elsie Montgomery, and Ruth L. Snyder with additional new material

CONTRIBUTORS & EDITORS

Alan Anderson lives in a small village called Deroche, British Columbia, with wife, Terry, and their poodle buddy, Charlie. He finds pleasure in practicing photography as a hobby. He especially likes to photograph eagles. Alan also enjoys walking on a local dike, where he finds much of the inspiration for his writing. He contributed stories to *Good Grief People* by Angel Hope Publishing, 2017, and *Story by Story: The Power Of a Writer*, Unstoppable Writers Publishing, 2018. Alan has also written articles for *FellowScript* Magazine and is a regular contributor to the InScribe Christian Writers' Fellowship blog. His personal Blog: https://scarredjoy.ca

Tandy Balson was born and raised in the Greater Vancouver area of British Columbia. She and her husband now live on the outskirts of Calgary, Alberta, close to their children and grandchildren. Tandy has discovered the insights that come from looking at life from a different perspective and shares those through the written and spoken word. She has published four books of short devotion/inspirational stories. As an inspirational speaker, she has spoken from coast to coast in Canada, and (with the help of an interpreter) in Mexico. Find out more at www.timewithtandy.com

Lorraine Boerchers finds refreshment and inspiration while enjoying nature, particularly the mountains. She finds the mountains soothing as they remind her of the majesty of God. A mountain view on the way to Costco, is there anything better? Lorraine has learned to carry a notebook and pens with her, as she never knows when creativity will strike! With God's nudging she is devoting more time to writing and sharing her poetry. Lorraine and her family live on an acreage south of Calgary.

Author **Janey Bordihn** is constantly finding beauty in everyday life, choosing to discover lessons in every moment she experiences. Mother of three grown children and living in Newmarket, Ontario, with her husband and golden doodle, she seeks to write compelling, thoughtful pieces on her discoveries throughout life's journey never failing to notice the humour, joy, and depth to life and faith that comes when we're open to finding it.

Whitney Braun is a through and through country girl with a passion for writing fiction. Her experiences of growing up in a British Columbia farm town provide unlimited inspiration for her stories. She currently resides on an acreage with her husband and son outside of her hometown of Fort St. John, British Columbia.

Phil Callaway is the best-selling author of over 30 books (including *Laughing Matters, Making Life Rich Without Any Money* and *Laugh Like a Kid Again*). Phil's humorous stories on family life have been featured in hundreds of magazines worldwide. His video series "The Big Picture" has been shown in 77,000 churches. Phil hosts the daily show Laugh Again, which airs on 300+ radio stations. He's a popular speaker for corporations, churches, and conferences. Phil and Ramona live within driving distance of their three kids and 16 grandkids. One of them said, "Bumpa. You're funny. I'm gonna keep you.

- www.philcallaway.com
- Subscribe to Laugh Again Radio at www.laughagain.ca
- Booking Info at bookphilc@gmail.com

Graeme Connell is a former journalist, public relations writer, and entrepreneur whose career has taken him from his native New Zealand to Antarctica, the Fiji Islands, the United States, and Canada.

Today he lives with his artist wife, Lois, in Calgary, Alberta, Canada, where he is never far away from his daughters, grandchildren, and great-grandchildren. His current novel-in-progress follows the novels *Layers* (2022), *Beginnings at the End of the Road* (2019), *Uncharted* (2016*), Finding Dermot* (2014), and memoir *Tide Cracks and Sastrugi* (2011).

Jeanelle Derry spent her summers herding her dad's cows, imagining the clouds forming different shapes. What was her shape? As a Special Education teacher and an avid reader, she had no desire to write until she met author Carol Kent at a conference. She asked her, "Carol, why would I want to write?" Looking Jeanelle right in the eye she responded, "How else would you let the creative out?" Carol's words stirred Jeanelle's soul. Writing allows God to share His promises in a real way while He forms and molds her.

L. Marie Enns was an eager student, avid reader, and enthusiastic singer. In her youth she wrote a few poems, but when she retired from teaching, and her children were grown, her writing increased. Joining InScribe Christian Writers' Fellowship was very helpful. Mostly, she writes poems and devotionals. Her work has been published in *FellowScript*, anthologies, the *Messenger*, *Esprit*, *Northern Pride*, and *The Senior Paper*. She also wrote *Preacher's Kids on the Homestead* and compiled her and her dad's writings in *Meditations*. Marie and Henry celebrated their 65th Wedding Anniversary in 2023. They have 4 children, 5 grandchildren, and 3 great-grandchildren.

Shannon Erickson is a marketer, photographer, and writer. She is passionate about creating in many ways, including photography, graphic design, and the written word. Born and raised in Saskatchewan, she returned in 2017 after living many years in Toronto and now lives in Yorkton with her family. Shannon is inspired by how much beauty there is in the detail of creation around us. She finds joy in capturing this beauty through macro photography. Her images invite the viewer into a meditative moment to quietly contemplate the natural wonders found in the tiniest details, continually changing with each season.

Scott Fitzsimmons is a radio professional, who spent over 20 years in the broadcast industry. In May 2019, he was diagnosed with Acute Lymphoblastic Leukemia. Soon after being cancer free, he began losing his sight. He then traded his microphone in for a pen, figuratively speaking. Scott's first full book (not done yet) is a memoir, documenting the ups and downs of his cancer journey. He also has plans for a handful of future projects. Scott lives in Yorkton, Saskatchewan with his beautiful wife, Sharlene, and three amazing kids, Sadie, Jackson, and Owen.

Barbara Fuller has been writing since she was a teenager. She has published four Bible studies, played with poetry, edited newsletters, composed articles, and—as an ordained minister—she has written many sermons. Barb blogs occasionally and is working on a memoir. She raised her three children in Nova Scotia and loves sharing adventures with her six delightful granddarlings. Her own adventures have taken her to ministry in Toronto, Ontario missionary service in Moldova, and grandparenting in Kamloops, British Columbia. Now that she is semi-retired, she has joined a writing group, and is finally reading the books on her shelves while she learns how to be a writer. Music, languages, and dogs bring her joy, but her heart is fullest walking with Jesus on a Nova Scotia beach. Find her books and her blog at www.barbarafullerauthor.wordpress.com

Writing and learning are happily married in **Pat Gerbrandt's** mind. Term papers—fun! She covered community news for the local newspaper and wrote one-page devotionals for a denominational paper. New friendships resulted from interviewing seniors for "Senior Focus," a *Christian Week* column. Writing/editing for *Canadian Home Trends* (home décor and lifestyle) was an eye-opening experience. Now, she focuses on memoirs, devotionals (*The Upper Room*), and *FellowScript* articles. Pat rereads favourite books but none as often as the Bible.

Family time, coffee or tea with friends, walking, doing crossword puzzles, making cards, sewing, and photography leave no room for boredom.

Marion Grace began her writing and ministry in response to the amazing love and power of God shown to her through some of life's most severe trials. She shares what God did and the principles He taught her to overcome, thrive, and become more than a conqueror. Marion's approach is always personal, transparent, real, and raw with a no-nonsense practicality that will speak to your heart and your situation. Marion lives in Nova Scotia, Canada, with her husband Steve and has three children and four grandchildren.

Lorilee Guenter is a Saskatoon-based writer and artist. She enjoys gardening, reading, and mentoring ladies young and old. She enjoys traveling near and far, including Sunday afternoon drives, hiking, and flying to distant cities. Lorilee admits she would rather relax at a campground after a hike than dodge crowds in a big city. She knows inspiration can be found everywhere. Sometimes it takes getting lost on vacation to find the jewel God has prepared for you. Contact her at lori@untroubled.org Maybe she will tell you how she knows about the value of taking an unexpected turn on vacation.

As a speaker, published author, and storyteller, **Carol Harrison** is passionate about mentoring people of all ages and abilities to help them find their voice and reach their fullest potential. She shares from her heart, through her writing and speaking, telling stories from real life experiences and God's Word to encourage people and help them find a glimmer of hope no matter what the circumstances. You can find more information at www.carolscorner.ca or email her at carol@carolscorner.ca

Colleen Jantzen is a Jesus-loving wife, mom, grandma, gardener, animal lover, hiker, knitter, quilter, baker, preacher, caregiver, life celebrant, and writer who is drawn to themes of grief, lament, the natural world, and calling the church to be kinder. Prose is her favourite genre to write in. Colleen has an essay published in *Looking Back, Leaning Forward: Wrestling with a Church's Story.* She's published in the *Ambrosia* Literary Review and an online magazine called *Ladies Corner*, but most of her work can be found on her blog at colleenrjantzen.ca and in her podcast at https://podcasters.spotify.com/pod/show/colleen-jantzen

Ruth Keighley has authored three books and numerous articles and coauthored one book. She loves hand embroidery, reading, jigsaw puzzles, and journaling for her grandchildren. She lives with her husband in Warman, Saskatchewan. This year, they celebrate their 50th anniversary. They have three children, ten grandchildren, and one great-grandson.

Starla Klinger is a believer, military spouse, mother, and writer who works part-time in communications. Growing up she created stories and began writing as an outlet for her feelings, questions, ideas, and prayers. As an adult her faith and life experiences are often the themes for her stories and devotionals. For her, writing brings calm and creativity into an often busy and change filled life.

Maureen E Kowal writes poetry and children's stories. She finds as she walks with God, the words flow across the paper. At the God Uses Ink Conference, 1998, she joined The Word Guild. She met June Stevenson, editor of *Glad Tidings*, a Presbyterian Missionary magazine and wrote poetry for them. Lynda Knight on The Word Guild posted for writers for The Fred Phonogram Series of The Perfection Learning Company. With help from Nancy J. Lindquist, Glynis Belec, Elma Schemenauer, she was published in two Grade One Vowel books *The Candy Map* and *The Loud Chime*. Maureen also writes poetry for Mary-Ellen Grisham, editor of *Eternal Ink* ezine magazine.

Tracy Krauss is an award winning and best-selling novelist, playwright, and artist with more than thirty books in print. Her work strikes a chord with those looking for thought provoking faith-based fiction laced with romance, suspense, and humor. She has a B.Ed. from the University of Saskatchewan and has lived in many remote and interesting places in Canada's far north. She and her husband currently reside in beautiful Tumbler Ridge, British Columbia, where she continues to pursue all of her creative interests. http://tracykrauss.com Contact: tracy@ tracykrauss.com ***"Fiction on the edge—without crossing the line"***

Inspired by the beauty of God's world around her, **Brenda Leyland** writes from her home in northerly Alberta, Canada. A long-time member of InScribe, she has been a columnist and contributor to *FellowScript* magazine. She sees herself as a curator of memories and blogs about her life at *It's A Beautiful Life* beautiful.wordfromhome.com Having nurtured a lifelong love affair with books and reading, she hopes her home in the next life has a cozy library with nooks and crannies stuffed to the rafters with the beautiful books she never had a chance to read in this life.

Sally Meadows is an award-winning author of children's books and short fictional stories; a four-time national award nominated singer/songwriter; and a non-fiction contributor to writing magazines and anthologies such as *Freelance, FellowScript, Chicken Soup for the Soul,* and the *Hot Apple Cider* series. She delights in sharing her work at author readings for kids and adults, as well as speaking at writing workshops and conferences. Sally was the recipient of InScribe's Barnabas Award in 2019 and the Janette Oke Award in 2020. Sally loves creating with paper and has enjoyed capturing God's creation across Canada with her camera.

Lorrie Morales is a semi-retired educator and grandmother who fell in love with writing, reading, and teaching at a young age. To this day, she dabbles in education, reads a plethora of books, and is a published author. If she isn't travelling, socializing, or walking, she is spending time with family, friends, or volunteering. You can find her with a smile on her face, enjoying the blessings life has to offer. You can follow her on Instagram @lorrie.morales.author, or check out her Blog and website at www.lorriemorales.com

Nina Faye Morey, B.A., B.Ed., is a writer, editor, artist, and speaker. She's contributed to three previous InScribe anthologies: *7 Essential Habits of Christian Writers* (2015), *Christmas: Stories & More* (2017), and *Easter: Stories & More* (2021). She's had fiction, nonfiction, poetry, and artwork published in numerous magazines and a column, *Editor Phobia*, in InScribe's *FellowScript* magazine. She's a former recipient of InScribe's Barnabas Award and previous editor-in-chief of *FellowScript*. Currently, Nina is InScribe Press Coordinator, Managing Editor of this anthology, and columns editor for *FellowScript*. She's contributed to the *InScribe Writers Online* blog and facilitated InScribe workshops. She enjoys walking, reading, travelling, and *Refreshing Your Creativity* at https://writerinkwell.weebly.com

Gail Neumann lives on the West Coast of British Columbia, near her children. Her writing has appeared regularly in local publications. She loves swimming and hiking and being out in nature. Multiple journals filled with daily prayers and responses are her passion. She has more writing projects on the go than she can ever seem to finish.

Marnie Pohlmann currently writes from a small town in Saskatchewan close to her grandchildren. She joins her husband, Wally, in Transitional Ministry for churches between pastors and does occasional transcription work, some basic editing, and bookkeeping. Her favourite downtime activities are reading, doing puzzles, board games, and playing with toy bricks. Marnie is writing a variety of pieces but really just likes to play with words.

Born and raised in Edmonton, Alberta, **Heidi Richardson** later married a farmer and left the city life. Now tucked away on a farm northwest of Calgary, Heidi loves to tell stories, but she often says, "If there is a bright center to the publishing universe, I'm on the planet it's furthest from!" (Apologies to George Lucas and Star Wars fans!) Through the decades, she's seen technology change from laborious pen and paper to today's swift computers. Now she writes fictional fantasies for young readers, where her creative dreams weave with biblical truths to create allegorical visions.

Valerie Ronald sees the world as a story waiting to be written, stemming from a passion for words since childhood. After graduating from Vancouver's Langara College journalism program, she worked as a newspaper reporter, bookstore employee, and public speaker. Her devotionals and articles have appeared in *Mennonite Brethren Herald, The Upper Room, FellowScript Magazine, Easter Stories & More,* and *InScribe Writers Online* blog. For a decade, she wrote weekly devotionals for an online blog, Scriptor Deus (scriptordeus.wordpress.com) Presently, she is compiling a book of 20 years of monthly devotionals written for her church bulletins. She and her husband live on the Canadian prairies, keeping in touch with their blended family and 10 grandchildren. Along with writing, Valerie enjoys nature photography, watercolour painting, and playing Scrabble.

Lynn J. Simpson is a writer, editor, and certified professional life coach who understands the need for creating spaces for rest, renewal, and transformation. She writes stories to inspire hope and is rarely without a camera in hand to capture breathing spaces to share. She's contributed to *Short and Sweet Too* (Grace Publishing, 2017), various anthologies, and published *Breathing Spaces: A 21-Day Journal of Rest, Reflection and Renewal* and *30-Day Journal of Thankfulness, Success & Joy*. http://www.LynnJSimpson.com

Ruth L Snyder is a Wall Street Journal bestselling author, international speaker, publisher, and CEO of RLS Creativity where we help faith-based entrepreneurs who are advancing the Kingdom of God to share their gifts and books with the world without forfeiting their souls. Publishing books; transforming lives! Ruth has shared her expertise on platforms like Thrive Global, Women in Publishing, Authority Magazine, The Global Interview, The Write Coach, Christian

Book Academy, and Girl Power Alliance. Connect with Ruth at https://linktr.ee/ruthlsnyder

Sandi Somers is a former teacher and Instructor of English as a Second Language, having taught in Alberta, South Africa, and Colombia, South America. Her devotionals and award-winning inspirational articles have appeared in various publications. Currently, her writing passion is sharing how God reveals Himself to us in both small and strategic ways. Sandi also enjoys reading, nature walks, gardening in season, and connecting with friends and extended family. She writes from her home in Calgary, Alberta.

Michelle Strutzenberger is the author of two non-fiction books, *Surprised by Grief and God* and *Growing Up in a Missionary Family of 10.* She has also published a children's book, *The Secret Talent Shop of Pineapple River.* She enjoys writing for *InScribe Writers Online* blog, and she was thankful for the opportunity to submit a column called the Weeble Diaries to *FellowScript Magazine* recently. She hopes and prays her written words bless and encourage those who read them. She can be reached at awakehopetoday@gmail.com

Carol Thornton is an Albertan but spent 15 years in the United Kingdom where she studied poetry at Oxford and with England's Poet Laureate, Andrew Motion. Her work has been published in Canada, the United States, England, Ireland, and Romania (in translation), and she was long-listed for the CBC Poetry Prize. She is co-author of *Writer on Fire: Poetry Prompts to Ignite the Poet Within* and is currently working to complete a creative non-fiction manuscript.

Raised in rank atheism, **Meg Tysoe** put her writerly passions on hold to study science. But God has a great sense of humour; He used nuclear physics and paleontology to open her mind and heart to the truth. Meg has been a radiation protection inspector, a flautist, a ghostwriter and developmental editor, a missionary speaker and writer, and a hopelessly romantic wayfarer. Most vitally, she is a mother and—along with her son and C. S. Lewis—a great lover of cats. Her new book, *More*

Than Stardust, confronts feeble beliefs with the power and intimacy of our triune Creator.

MaryAnn Ward resides in Regina, Saskatchewan, with her husband of over fifty years. Condo living and "retirement" has released this wife, mother, and grandmother, to the full-time pursuit of author, illustrator, publisher, and prophetic artist. Bible teaching, speaking, and pastoral ministry round out any free time. Her latest book, *Thursday's Child Has Far to Go,* is a vulnerable memoir, offering healing and hope to both the wounded and wounders of sexual addiction. Discover more at https://maward.ca/

Irene Worster-LoScerbo loves tinkering with language, colour, sounds, and situations, and is happiest when God reveals connections between things that appear totally unrelated. Whether she uses words or photo-art to connect the dots He provides, Irene's desire is that the result pleases and praises the Great Author-Creator. Reach Irene at solonoi@shaw.ca